PARENTAL CURSE

THE CHAINS OF INCESTUOUS SLAVERY (THE PHYSICAL EFFECTS)

Bethonie Rose

BALBOA.
PRESS
A DIVISION OF HAY HOUSE

Balboa Press books may be ordered through booksellers or by contacting:

Balboa Press
A Division of Hay House
1663 Liberty Drive
Bloomington, IN 47403
www.balboapress.com.au
1 (877) 407-4847

Print information available on the last page.

ISBN: 978-1-5043-1637-8 (sc)
ISBN: 978-1-5043-1638-5 (e)

Balboa Press rev. date: 01/08/2019

You will behave how I want you to behave!

"I will carve out the perfect life for me from my personal perspective," said the sexual molester.

"Then you got here [unspoilt gentle soul]! And there were so many other dysfunctional people around you who had already lost sight of their own guidance system of what is right and wrong.

"Then they said to you, gentle soul, 'I am very conditioned as a love giver and liver of life.'

"This means good conditions make *me* [sexual molester] feel good, while bad conditions make me feel bad.

"So these are my rules for you, my sexual victim, for the good conditions I need to exact from you, and since you're in my life, I will be looking at you quite a lot since I am your sexual predator leech!

"And when I look at you, I want to feel good, which means you need to perform in ways that make *me, me, me, me, me, me, me* feel good. I don't want you to be selfish!

"You, my victim, need to behave in ways that make me, your selfish caregiver [from the mentally disturbed child molesting family], feel good! If I see any of those things that make me feel bad, you will be in such trouble.

"Now, this would be all right if they were the only dysfunctional persons in your life and they were all in agreement with themselves.

"But they are so fickle, and there are so many of them, all wanting different things from you, and you just can't stand on your head in enough different ways to make them [all the people in your life] happy. Pretty soon you'll figure out that no matter how hard you try, you can't make them happy!"

The biggest hypocrisy, the thing that's caused me the biggest trouble, is that they (parents, brother, sexual predators, caregivers) all tell you that you are so important to them, but the bottom line is this: *How they feel is the most important thing to them.* Therefore, they keep trying to guide you and your behaviour by what makes them feel good.

You, however, are left feeling bad, left with resentment and a shattered life that takes years to repair and sort out, trapped in a mental prison that they have made for you.

— Bethonie Rose

1

CHAPTER

As a small child, you learn to accept whatever treatment is dished out to you. You never really know until later in life—when you begin to question the facts presented around you, analysing constantly—whether what you had experienced was at all correct and what a family is supposed to be. The propulsion of birth as you're crushingly pushed from the loving embrace of the soft, warm womb, imagining that, in reality, should not this be the worst of the pain you have to endure from this life in this family as the contraction of life squeezes you out into the cold new world? Your tiny body is held in the hands of others, and you are slapped into this world; the screams of realization to life spring forth. You have no control over any decisions that will be made, for your physical well-being is now held cradled in the arms of another.

My first real, significant dream was one of breathless terror. My sleeping moments were tormented nightly with visions of nil escape as the vivid images danced in my mind and stayed there for some twenty-five years—a life sentence of sorts. The same images played over and over, only slightly changing as the years went on. This was one of just three significant dreams that made up my existence and gave my life a structural scaffold to rebuild. What is the meaning of life and did my being born have a significant role in anything in this world? Or was I just a mistake, a cruel joke of such, meant to be tormented and left with little or no answers? I felt left isolated to endure the behaviour being dished out on a continuous basis. Was that all my life was going to be, a constant barrage of shitty episodes that would somehow sum up my life? Or was this a little different? Was I different? I was to discover the constant small images that made my nights difficult were the beginning of a journey of a thousand steps, all of which led to this one spot on which I now stand. I was about to embark on the final steps to this situation I found I was born into, but I was never really privy to the true family secrets held in this family vault.

I am staring into a society that says, "Do something," but even if we do something, will anything ever really change? Or is that just meant to keep us happy and held in suspension so we do not totally get out of hand? I now question the accountability of everyone as my journey of a thousand steps is coming to an end. I stand here with the realization that this world in which I live seldom holds anyone to any true accountability. No one truly makes amends, and we are just fodder to keep someone in a job. The whole thing that is life continues like nothing really matters in the whole goddam mess. The fingers of those social justice keepers are forever stuck in the proverbial dyke of mirrored, disillusioned bullshit we call life because we don't really wish to fix this mess and deal with anything. Is it that hard to fix the mess, or are we just all cowards refusing to look into the deep-seated heart of truth?

A span of fifty years of life—and really, what did it amount to? A life of struggle. Or was this a test to see if I would have the sheer guts and determination to place my life into the hands of the universe and see what was in store for me if I allowed the universe to mould my life? I have spent most of my life being on my own—truly on my own—even though people around me were saying they love me; but in my case, they never did; still I was left physically feeling alone. So *alone* is a funny word, considering we are surrounded by people. But really people like us; we are totally on our own in all this shit? This shitty existence of sorts begins with the question of why I was born at all, if all I got was nothing but a horrible feeling that there was something very wrong with me. This happened slowly at first—the not really talking to me and the separation away from the whole conglomerate that was family. Cruelness that comes from being subjected to punishment for a crime you will never commit but which you are held responsible for persecuted for the rest of your life. Physically, the response of such carefully manoeuvred behaviour is of such slightness that over the years, one conclusion was reached that seemed logical: there must be something really wrong with me!

The setting of your foundational generational pillar stones that you will stand on for life takes place before you are even aware that you have a body, and the tiny fingers are set on a course of destruction that takes years to escape. The family—as I was encouraged to believe I belonged to—was the only thing that really mattered. As the years passed, the attitudinal differences would become more and more prominently brought to my attention as my attitude being so very wrong. A comment here and there, with no real comprehension, goes unnoticed, but as the years of deliberate layering of false accusatory mud sticks and the rusty decay sabotages the foundation on which you stand, the years start to take their toll. The digging, my relentless search for answers in this foundational quicksand, would eventually bring this crumbling house to ruin. The realization of the corrupting hand for which I was born to rest in that day of my birth would be made oh so very real. The cleverly crafted words and the deliberately withheld affection would all be held under a magnifying glass of analysing until the final piece to my life's puzzle would be placed in the cavernous erosion in my heart and the whole picture of my life could be looked upon. The meaning of life … *What does it means to be treated so mean?*

The small blank canvas of my body was unblemished at birth. The supposed loving hands of the artists who are your parents begin to sculpt the essence that will comprise your self-esteem. Through your mind's eye, you now hold this image of yourself, the guiding light of whether you're held special, true, and deserved within the boundaries of this family. The caressing of the body in the arms of loved ones fills the heart and helps to develop the first chakra foundational point in this person whole life as they hold in their hands the ground you stand on.

The holding of a baby is of special significance, as it's here that the moulding of the person and his or her significance in this world begins. Are babies special enough to behold love and be shown real, tender heart care? Or has this one unblemished small child been assigned another fate? Experts say a child will die if he or she is not shown affection or held in loving arms. This comes to mind now regarding the way I was programmed. I was constantly told of an experiment done by scientist's years ago. Was I also being experimented on by my family for a similar purpose? Was this a way to self-discriminate as having no real accountability for the path they had set for me? Was this the reason I was not cherished as a sacred member of this family?

Physical love for children is important. It gives them a sense of boundaries regarding what is right and wrong. It shows that their tiny bodies belong to them, and it shows how others should behave and treat them as they're taught and developing the boundary proximities that others should respect. They are developing a sense that they are special enough to warrant some protection under the cloak that is this family. The strong bonds of protection are created and instilled upon children while they are so young. They are trying to understand just how precious they are to this pack of people bound together in supposed love.

This results in the image these small people have of themselves, and whether they are worthy to have a place in this special world we call family. The physical touch—the patting, brushing of the hair, cuddling, sitting on laps, snuggling while bedtime stories are read—shows signs of someone being accepted into the fold and being allowed the special, significant place of family and being loved.

When the dreams started to appear, I was a mere child of eight who was not able to comprehend the significance of where I fitted into this tiny world of my family. The faceless figure was standing at the end of my bed. Knowing that there was no real escape, I think, was the first real knowledge of this dream. The small, helpless young girl was sitting on this bed in a room of a house, trapped and all alone. Knowing the helplessness, she woke up! It was not even my house; it was nothing like the house I grew up in but one conjured up in my dreams.

The small heart races as the disturbed sleep immobilizes you on your bed, the waking memories of the dream echoing the realization that you're alone. Within the cold and impersonal darkness of this lonely room, you hide under the covers, begging the covers to be enough to keep this formidable shadow person from harming you—until sleep once again leads you into unconscious thoughts. The integrated complexities of this dream are incomprehensible for many, many years to come.

The intermingling of the self-esteem with the physical appearance is all too much to understand for an eight-year-old girl whose hallowed existence in this family had already begun to be something of a scapegoat-like dilemma for her. From such a young age, I had already been subjected to the cruelness of my somewhat older brother. Physical scars can be easily seen and fixed up, covered over as just childish fun gone wrong. Everything is fun until someone gets hurt, which was usually me. It was supposed to be quickly forgotten, with life moving at such a fast pace that we cannot stop to hold accountable anything that we should. The family carpet begins to be woven as the dust of corrupt thinking blows in, sweeping it out of sight and forgotten. We are to move on. But what if the physical scars you have are ones that you were encouraged to bury, forged when comprehension of such experience has been savagely ripped from one's ownership control, never to be enjoyed by the person's growing mind, gone just such a precious thing, lost and forever vanished? It is forcibly buried deep in the foundational existence of your life and continuously affecting everything thereafter, prolonging the pain long after the prison wardens of your childhood release you from their superior clutches.

I try to keep in my mind a vision of an elegant woman who holds herself with such grace and poise. I wait in the lounge in my apartment on the floating ship, wearing an elegantly designed white outfit that streamlines my shapely body perfectly, waiting for my partner to pick me up for dinner. I sit waiting for my man who adores me to escort me to dinner on the exclusive cruise ship where we are privileged to own a private suite. These ever so delicate loving hands cradle my cherished heart forever, vigilant not to drop it or hurt it. He tenderly takes my hand in his and gently escorts me to my seat as I hold myself with such poise and grace.

The memories of my childhood existence are a faded wisp now that only occasionally appear if triggered, but they are quickly dismissed as now being wrong, as my image of the once- tormented girl's eyes no longer stare back at me from the mirror. I think this is one of the reasons I never gave up in my search for true answers and self-worth understanding, for I was waiting for this version of myself, as the elegant woman dressed in white, to appear when I looked into the mirror of life. This is how I would like to see myself now in my mind's eye of self-esteem, rather than the once-held mirror image that stared back at me from behind tormented eyes. The small girl of tender years damaged, ugly, and unloved, disregarded by her family as nothing more than a sexual play toy for her older brother to experiment on. The image of my persona I held in my mind, the one that I had held on to for many years, burned indelibly in my heart and got closer to becoming a reality the deeper I healed from my incestuous hell.

After many years of working on myself, the results now show a person with confidence and poise, one who knows that she is of top-shelf value. This is a far cry from the imaginings my mother was trying to instil with her words of "clean up your brothel," the words still ringing in my mind of this phrase intended to mould my tender character to match the illusion instilled in my mother's mind by my father and brother—that I was to blame for being abused sexually by her oh-so-beautiful boy. The courageous fight fought on the social battlefield of life was to obtain my image I had of myself and not be tricked into the prostitutional wanting of my family, which would allow them the clear conscious persona they held of me. They were forever blaming me, claiming that this was my fault and not a result of their own disgusting behaviour that allowed this to take place under their roof. I was triumphant that I had turned out the way I intended and not the programmed cheap whoring woman, drug dependent on men, persona intended by them.

The image was so carefully crafted and moulded to represent them as pillars of the community, which is what they wanted the town to think they were. These were false representations of what was actually there. I sit here knowing that not many will ever really know what it was like to live in a family such as mine. But then there were those who held this illusion of my family in high stead, the ones who still think that my father was a good man. My God, this must be wrong—she has to be lying—and well, it's just preposterous to think this was going on under his roof; he must not have known!

Still, to this day, forty years later, fully knowing and going through the experience myself with the court case pending, I still cannot get my head around the fact that they knew! They knew exactly what was going on and chose to say nothing but to simply ignore the goings goings-on under their own roof! The cherished illusion was a better fit in their lives than to stop and face what was actually happening within the confinement of the family. Their son, their precious son, was allowed to sexually abuse his sister, with no family boundary restraint voiced. There was no comprehension of the secret laws broken and the free hand flippantly waved of consent as their blind eye blinked in approval. I can still hear the police constable saying to me, "What a complete dickhead—he knew from almost day one what was going on and did nothing to stop it." The disbelief in his voice was evident while he was struggling to get his mind around the fact that both my parents knew exactly what their outstanding son was doing to their daughter, held down from grace, and did nothing to stop it!

I started to write this almost at the end of the saga, which for me, as you now know, started, when I was quiet young. But it has spanned my lifetime, the sheer betrayal, hidden forbidden truths, as well as prolonged trained self-deception, which is when many turn to drugs or alcohol to help cope with the crippling confusion from which most never recover and escape. Some choose to turn to the blissful comfort of suicide, to escape the mind torture spinning uncontrollably in their memory banks day after day. Some choosing to go down the path of least resistance and accept the path chosen for them and prostitute themselves in life, I did not. I was born under Chiron, the deep wound healing planet, and I was never allowed to go down that path of self-destruction but edged ever so confusingly and sometimes forcefully into a situation that gave me back my self-respecting personal power. This is my story, something that *no one* can ever steal from me.

2
CHAPTER

The physical scars are all but hidden from the world now, only due to the fact that they are not seen or understood by the seer. I will try to explain the affect it's had on my life and how the skills I have had to develop helped me to cope and deal with all my abuse still lingering in my cell memory to this day. Wrapped up within the fabric of three dreams which helped me unlock the aspects of my soul, allowing me to take possession once again, my clawing back to the light from the blackened abyss in which my family shoved me. I find that people don't care much unless something unbearable is happening to them, and then they are all ears so they can get a glimpse of how to speed up their healing so the pain will go away, forever thankful that their pain is made easier from the pain of struggle I endured. But alas, when it comes to this type of affliction scar, it is difficult to see how it affects this person. But to the inherent recipient, the guilt we try to hide screams out from our bodies in crying shame.

But the scars are there, and here I will try to explain just what happens to you as your tiny body contorts itself into locking away the guilt and shame within the lower vertebra of your spine as you compact the anger that you are forbidden to express but forced to take ownership of. This compacting of the unexpressed anger energy the body deposits in the second chakra centre, which is where the foundational principle energy of relationships with yourself and other people resides. As the abuse continues to rob you of your self-respect, these principles are distorted to allow the family its uncontested law breaking behaviour. You store this corrupting energy in the lower part of your spine, held there until the body is unable to keep it there any longer. Or the escaping of blissful suicide is achieved, whichever comes first. This excessive now-trapped energy begins to exploit your hips in a balloonish way, leaving your buttocks and hips storing the trapped energy and distorting them, making them larger than they otherwise should be. I still see the astonished expression, only matched by their amazement, of people who have not seen me for some time when they say, "You have changed so much. What's happened to you?" The once excessively swollen hip region of my body is now gone, as the effects of the trapped, twisted, and tormented physical energies have now escaped.

The addictions you scramble to secure as a child, to help keep all this trapped energy in its acceptable place, begin to develop and take over your life as you breathlessly see your future slip into the deep well of despair. My overeating issues began, which I find many sexual abuse victims have, so this energy of anger being produced does not express itself—the forbidden expressing of pain and the held in tears all stuffed down with another serving of ice cream! It was the chosen heroin of an eight-year-old girl, just to name the first of sometimes many addictions one will employ in an attempt to stop these forbidden sins from being expressed, which may hurt the hearer of non-responsibility. And the substances which may help one feel normal.

The realization of a life so scarred began its physical sexual exploits at such a young age, to be completely over by the age of fifteen. I would be interested when you look back at my life and try to pinpoint where this all started, evaluating the exact moment he was allowed to take possession of my physical body and begin to corrupt the fabric of my soul. I think I was about three when he soon learned that from action, which usually meant his on me, from which there should have been consequences, that there were none. He was free to manipulate any punishment he chose on me. At four years old, I don't think you fully comprehend the world. Or maybe it was the fact that I was just so young, which may be the reason I find those memories all but gone. Or maybe memories are forged from significant events that are so pivotal they cannot help but be but scorched on to your mind and vibrational soul forever.

I have a memory of being pushed out of a tree and hurtling down about two metres hard onto a path below, splitting my head open as the impact was felt and blood came rushing. My brother's desire to be the centre of attention that day was far too great to subdue, as his need for being king of the world won and jealousy of me grew in him.

I don't think the branch my brother enticed me onto would have held any weight, let alone mine, as he promised it would. I recall the screams of my cousins, who ran off to find my parents to help with the clean-up and recovery of my broken head, as well as the blood-soaked towel hanging over the bathtub. I think the stitches were the reward of that little incident, the first of many accidents that were bestowed upon me by my sadistic brother, for which he was never punished, heaven forbid. Maybe that's why I turned to religion for a while, to try to make sense of all this muddled confusion. So maybe that's where it started. I am not sure, but as the years went on, the sadistic cruel behaviour got worse, as you will see. I found that I truly had little hope of ever having the wonderful life many little girls grow up having.

Next to come was being pushed off the trampoline and smashing into the ground, which soon left me with the reality of pain once again, as my tiny bones in my arm were shattered when it made contact with the earth. I was plastered up for weeks as my little bones in my arm repaired, focussing more on the decorating of the plaster cast on my broken arm rather than the crime from which it was made! He got no smacked bum, just got away with doing that to me also. A pattern was starting to emerge. He did not have an audience that day, so maybe he just saw an opportunity and took it, the forging of an attitude that became a staple of his personality. There were extremely vivid memories of aching bones and racing in the car to the next significant town to be patched up.

Then there was the large bull ant's nest that was beside the rotary hoe that had been sitting for many years outside the house on the farm. With his encouragement, we threw stones at it. I was bitten by many of them as they came to defend their home from attack—funny that. It was about then that I started to see how I was a burden for my mother, who was content with scolding me rather than comforting me as she dabbed my swollen hurting body with vinegar, saying that I deserved this, that it served me right. There were no frills and whistles, just the facts, because that's all I knew. I was about four and a half, maybe five, when all that happened.

I often found my mother to be a very cold and unloving person. I cried the day my astrologer said to me, when viewing my spiritual chart for the first time, "Your mother was an utter bitch to you, and your father was a mongrel bastard." My body's self-posturing was in automatic defence, collapsing when the realization that this person knew just what I had had to endure and I no longer needed to prop it up in defence to hide. Someone else could truly see the way it must have been for me in this family.

The little girl who sat on that bed in my dreams was finally being heard. The dreaming state world where she was a prisoner of her world in her dreams but also mirrored my real world of reality as well was finally starting to emerge from the covers of darkness. The house that was constructed in my first dream was rather large and was built on the banks of a large lake in the middle of nowhere. It was a quiet, secluded area of the world, with no real visitors and no one to play water sports on the lake, just a cold and empty place that no one had discovered. The room I resided in was small, with louvers halfway up the wall to the ceiling, all made of glass and spanning the length of the room. This room never changed, even in wintertime, when the lake would ice over and the cold winds came in. I lived in this one room for the years that the first dream persisted, this small room that only seemed to have a bed in it, hanging out into the water on stilts, with no way of escape out the window for fear of falling into the watery depths below.

Over the years, the anger and frustration of my real world found its way into my dream world, causing her to lose what little control of her life she had. The more control over my environment that I lost in my real world, the more she lost in my dreaming world. The two worlds became inseparable. As the two worlds combined, the supposed reality of my two worlds became distorted. The small girl of my dreams became more and more controlled and trapped within the existence of her world. The then-nightly attempts of escape became a challenge as the darkness of sleep stole her into unconsciousness. By then, the figure of my dreams had complete possession of my life and her world outside this house was gone. Her eyes were staring out of her window over the lake, forever desiring escape from this world; the only freedom from this room and her life were the visions that escaped through her sight.

The ability to rely on this family for any protection evaporates as the controlling family member manoeuvers its players, like a conductor of an orchestra. Your trust in the family is dissolved, and then, little by little, your trust in yourself goes as the corrupting lies are replaced where your truth once belonged. The trust to trust your decisions is so eroded and non-existent and the eyes with which you now look out are forced to distort what you're actually seeing. The once-truthful environment is replaced with carefully crafted lies that hold your accountability of a situation in the mistrustful words of your family—ever so quickly corrected if the truth is unearthed by accident and the shameful light shone on your parents. You question whether these people love you, and common sense says that they should. You are flesh of their flesh, or you think you are, but you question what you are seeing, and what is happening to you, as wrong is made right all the time. It's a constant conflict you face on a regular basis, fighting daily to justify the behaviour of your family. You are constantly shut down with comments that you are seeing things wrongly, being told that if you would only change your attitude, that your attitude to the way you perceive you're being treated is wrong.

One such occasion when blatant disregard for good parenting by my caregiver went out the window was displayed when I got a golf ball in the face. Yes, I mean a golf ball flung full pelt at my face, hitting me on the cheek and almost breaking the cheekbone on the right side. I can still feel the sheer impact of that object hitting me in the face and the excruciating pain that emerged as the resulting swelling and throbbing pain ensued. The stream of memories come flooding back to me now, having fun, only to be confronted by a father of little self-control and full of malice. To throw a golf ball at his daughter's face because she had taken the centre of attention off him and innocently drawn it to herself—what a crime!

Being treated as such, you begin to fall from grace and begin to see the treatment of yourself, of such cruelty and such disrespect, as commonplace, but what power do you have to change what is happening to you? You step out of line and mistakenly think your self-esteem could go up a notch, but again you are reminded to stay in that box. Shaming the family was the greatest of sins, as you were rewarded with floggings until you could not sit down, the punishment carried out at the boss man's discretion. So you begin to lose sight, not able to care how you are treated, as the years of being treated badly are just too many to fight anymore. You now know it is commonplace to be treated so badly that you stop questioning whether you deserve this behaviour, as that is the only behaviour that is served up to you. Physically, I was a bigger girl, bigger than my older brother was, but he was taller and physically stronger due to being much older than I was. "Big-boned" was the expression back then, which was used to describe my physique, but now, with many years of understanding behind me, I now know that my body structure was different from the others in my family.

In the world, there are two body structures, depending on the energy that you are conceived with, from the seed of your father's lineage. You're conceived with either yang energy or yin energy, depending on the energy sequence that is held in the conceiving of that child. I have a yang body type, which means I have an outwardly expressed emotional vibration; my hips are large, my bum is shapely, and my boobs are large. A yin body type, which was what every member of my immediate family had, had an inwardly held emotional vibration, with narrow hips and thin stature. The two structures have different energies behind them, which means these types of people have different personalities from each other's structures. The yin types all vibrate to a particular frequency, thus having similar personalities. However, I belong to a different vibrational energy pattern from the rest of my family and thus behaved and valued things differently than the other members of this collective group did. This group which I called my family.

I suppose you would consider me the black sheep of my family, but truly, I was just a different type of sensitive than other members of this family. In their eyes, my then-small number of skills to arm myself from these people was wrong—wrong in its delivery and expression and wrong in my justification that I should be allowed to have any cause to protect myself from them. They justified their behaviour as being correct, but in fact it was extremely incorrect morally in addition to being just plain cruel, as you will come to see. I was defenceless against this pack of reptilian bastards that had laid claim to my own Druidical system of what was right and wrong. They were trying to mould me in their corrupting ways so that their wrongs could be made right!

With this valuable key of knowledge, I was able to view things far clearer than I ever had. I did not have this understanding of the two different body structures until I was well in my thirties. It however allowed me to see things from a different perspective than the one I was once forced to have and embrace by my family. Up until then, although I already sensed that I held values quiet differently from other members of this family, I had no comprehension for the reasoning for being energetically different other than the fact that I saw things differently and thus reacted differently. At that young age, believing that I must have been adopted into this pack was the only reason at that young age that I could logically reason why I was treated with such nasty displeasurable behaviour by these people.

Learning of this structural difference held such a valuable key of knowledge triggered a series of events that allowed me to figure out why I was singled out for this persecution within my family, although it still took many years for this to be revealed. I never realized how it would unlock the reasoning behind my chosen fate that day I was born and why I had been singled out for such discrimination within this family. Ultimately, it was one of the key pieces that gave me such peace of mind; it was what I craved but had no idea I needed. The inevitable conclusion created many years before my birth singled me out to be crucified, to take blame for another's wrongdoing. It was placed clearly on my shoulders to deal with was this unspoken guilt, perhaps saving the responsible criminals from any moral reckoning. It was a reminder to my father of a crime committed a generation before that resulted in the vibrational patterning for another two generations to come. I was persecuted by my father's guilt, unbeknown to me, a silent reminder of what he himself had done to his own sister, my similar body structure sledgehammering his guilty heart. Every time he looked at me, his own daughter, his eyes were unable to avoid the reminder of what he had done to his own sister. His spiteful words fell from his lips regularly, saying that I reminded him of his sister, adding, "You're just like your auntie, the one I despise."

I would love to have answers to the questions that sometimes swim around my mind, unanswered by my mother, but the particles of her life now blow in the wind from the ashes that were once alive. I was never truly able to get answers and will definitely not get them from a man who still believes nothing wrong was done to me. His mind considered it only a few tiddlywinks, harmless touching rather than the full-blown sexual exploitation that it was—the setting up, the continued exploitation of the innocence stolen and paid forward to men who ill deserved it but thought it their God dame right to take possession of it, and squander it at their will.

Now my ability to distinguish a good foundation for relationships was gone, stolen, and something else was forcefully put into its place. My abuse spanned over the entirety of the second chakra sequencing time frame of seven years and thus affected all aspects of relationships for me over those seven years of patterning. So the foundational platform on which I needed to build my future life was very warped and malformed, having led a somewhat married existence with my brother, with no other relationship qualification other than sex being his only need, unless I had a possession he wanted of mine, whilst pushing me away and leaving me needy and emotionally starved for all other aspects of a somewhat married life. Why must something that was forced upon me leave me to have to deal with this affliction quietly on my own, with little to no help from my family? So the perpetrators get off free and have no real issues to have to suffer or deal with except the ones self-inflicted, while it leaves me having to deal with the results of others' behaviour for four decades and more, which energetically had been decided before I was born.

My mother was an out worldly quiet woman. In hindsight, I think it was because my father had iron rod control of the family so his perfect workaholic world wouldn't change and he could build his empire. It was evident from the constant floggings I got to make sure I was kept in line, reinforcing, at least in his mind, that I was the one to blame here. I struggled for many years with my mother's refusal to protect her daughter from this molesting that was being done to me, her own daughter, on a regular basis now. How could my mother just turn her heart into stone and repugnantly refuse to protect me all those years ago? Was it just too hard to stand up to a man who had such deluded thinking that he was in the right? Was the price for my justice far too steep for her to pay?

The first signs that something was wrong within my own children's lives and their situation turned me into a protective lioness eager to extrude my protective roar for all to see. Maybe at times it was a little too much protection for their liking, but after being through what I had endured, I could not see the problem in being a staunch protector of their precious self-esteem, so flippantly disregarded and crushed with parental right as mine was. So was it wrong of me to wish to protect them and make strong that which was constantly destroyed in me the moment it looked as if I was taking a stand and a surge of new comeback strength was standing in the way of my sexual abuses and the next conquest of my body?

I liken my childhood experiences in my family to a boxing match where you have been placed in the ring. You take your corner, your back against the ropes. Sitting on the stool, you gently turn your head to see who is in your corner. Help and support are there for you. They wipe the sweat off your brow and congratulate or sympathize with you. They rally to your side, patting you on the back and giving you positive energy exchange, communicating with common words and phrases that you have yourself used, in addition to the familiar vibration of shared collective. Soothing your tired battered body, the caressing of arms stretch out in peoples congratulations, as pats on the back of encouragement are exchanged. Oh, no, wait! That's my brother's corner, not mine.

I often think I had no one in my corner, as my parents clearly supported and cared for my brother's needs and comfort. I just knew that the loneliness of being totally on your own turns your bones into powder and leaves you unable to rely on anyone except yourself—no one to turn to, no one in your corner, just the knowing that you are there all alone. There's no hooray, no support, no person to catch you when you fall and envelop you with love, his or her warm and gentle arms caressing the hurt. Imagine for a moment being pushed off a cliff and hurtling down to the ground with no parachute or friends, only the knowledge you are about to hit the ground and there will be no one to help pick up your broken bones and put you back together again. There's just the desperate need to be saved from this misery so you can begin to heal, but you are never allowed to escape, as the abuse continues for years to come.

It's just you in a ring, which we will call family, having the shit beat out of you and never having anyone to hit that bell and say stop! You are tossed back into the corner when they have satisfied their need for sadistic cruelty. You lick your wounds by yourself and comfort the tiny bit of self-respect you have left as you climb back in your hole, the one which you are forced to dig out for yourself so you have a place to lick your wounds. You are puzzled at what triggered this latest flurry of insults, anger, and flogging abuse, stunned again that you fell into their trap and again were too helpless and vulnerable to protect yourself from these pack of thugs I called family.

There will be no champion parade, no heavyweight belt, no pats on the back for a job well done, the kisses and exhortation of fans telling you that they love you. You are just a tired and shattered shell of a body tired of fighting an unwinnable fight. You drag this body back to the hole that now resembles a jail rather than a soft place to fall, to begin again the painstaking ritual of putting your nakedly exposed self-esteem back together. This seemingly gets harder and harder every time you're forced to reconstruct it. You ready yourself for the next spine-shattering round in which again you will not win, and again you will wonder what the hell triggered it.

Over the years of honing my detective skills, I needed to sort this mess out; it dawned on me that I was the trigger. I was the trigger for the flurry of insults, abuse—sexual, mental, emotional, and physical—and everything else that could be dished out. There were the weeks of silence, being ignored, the lonely breakfasts by myself, the torment that I had committed some horrific crime for which my prison warden had put me in solitary for a month, until I showed signs of improved behaviour. I was repeatedly told that my aggressive behaviour would not be tolerated, that my attitude was all wrong, and that if I just changed my attitude, things would be better! Now what was that goddam attitude that I had but was unable to fathom as a ten-year-old? Just what the hell was this fucking attitude that I was supposed to change?

Many years later, it occurred to me that the pain I would soon have to endure in a dance of four-month intervals was triggered, I thought, by the unrelenting desire to stand up and be counted. My sprouting of newly developed self-esteem from the latest attempt at feeling normal enough to belong to this family had become too apparent for my captives, and I needed to be pushed back down into the very hole that they had made me retreat to months earlier. "Getting too big for your britches, young lady. You needed to be chopped down."

How dare I have enough strength to stand up to them? I needed to be made pliable in their hands, and the neglect, beatings, and segregation would start again. I would be left vulnerable and all alone. The venomous nastiness dripped from their mouths as the flurry of insults and bullying exploded. "Sticks and stones may break your bones, but words will never hurt you." What shit! I heard this whenever I complained of being continuously insulted, which was too much for me to contain in my tiny confused body, and I would verbalize it aloud. I was told this regularly as guardian support evaporated and parental consent of said behaviour continued. His desire to possess this next part of my soul was all too familiar to his captive now, his learned behaviour of how he could break down my boundaries of defiant behaviour towards him well practised.

In his eyes, he owned me, and he was now using his ability to crucify me in this family as a badge of honour. My now-weakened boundary state, with parental licence given to march over this, I was now weakened by segregation, loneliness, and shame, my flogging complete. My attitude needed changing and why couldn't we work together? I didn't wish to hear about it! I didn't want to know! You're such a pain in the ass. I was putty in his hands, the defiance now subdued as he marched onwards towards conquering his next platitude. I had been taught to endure my dance in the family, to stand up so they had the beautiful pleasure of knocking me back down like ten pins at the bowling rink. My mother so proudly told me one day that she hadn't wanted children, and I truly wish she had not had them.

I once heard of an experiment of a dog being placed in a cage, and when electrifying one side of the cage, the dog moved to the left. They electrified the left side, and the dog moved to the right. Again and again, the dog moved to the side of the cage that was not being electrified, until both sides of the cage were electrified. The dog stood there and wet himself because he knew he could not win, no matter what he did. This is how I felt many times when I was picking myself up and beginning to feel good again. I would be crushed again in the family boxing ring and left to lick my wounds in the corner. I often wished someone would rescue me from this and please make me understand why I had to endure this shit I was subjected to while living in this family from hell!

3

CHAPTER

It is somewhat hard to fathom just how the touching and the sexual play started because there was so much of it. I mean, how do you? Begin, to document such behaviour into comprehensible words when the sheer anguish of reliving it left me astounded at the level of control this young man was allowed to have over me. I do know, however, that my brother was like a spider enticing me into his web. For weeks, he would hit me and be very nasty to me, using insult after insult, disregarding his audience he had around him, crushing down the little self-esteem that I had managed to muster. Ignoring me was common practice in my family, making me very lonely and feel isolated, as though I had done something mysteriously wrong and deserved to be pushed away so as not to infect the others.

Then, as if it were a dance, he would start being nice to me, and I could not understand just what I had done to make him change his behaviour towards me as he began to draw me into his web. I was never able to distinguish just what I had done to warrant such nice behaviour from him. I was puzzled for days, my mind focusing on just what I had done. How could I continue having this person treat me so nicely? What had I had done to please this person in my family? The family curse had been broken again. What was it that I had done to make it so? *Oh, let me remember,* I thought, *so I can always behave in such a way.* I never found out because of my low self-esteem, and the roller-coaster ride of abuse would start again. The way my family treated me was a pattern of behaviour designed to keep me just where I was meant to be, crushed and down there. Theoretically, I should have stayed down there, where they kept putting me over and over again because that's what this level of abuse is designed to do. By that, I mean keeping you from being able to rise up and expose just what was happening in this supposed "loving family."

Many years passed before I said, "No more. Fuck off and leave me alone. You're not nice to me at all, you people who were my family." Whom else did I have? I was so young. It was a long time before I was strong enough to walk away from these reptilian beasts I was forced to call family. Either you suck it up and put up with this behaviour or you live on the streets—whichever choice you can endure, I suppose. So the next time you criticize someone for living on the streets or you see a prostitute, stop! Ask yourself why that person is there. Please don't turn a blind eye in unseeing ignorance, because you no longer can after reading this book, for you will now see just how this person came to be.

I was so innocent in my thinking but carefully manipulated and constructed over time to be snared like a little animal in a trap. What I do remember is my brother being especially nasty to me, and then, for no apparent reason, he would be incredibly nice to me and wish to spend time with me, enticing me into his room, which happened over a few days. We would play whatever game he wanted to play. It was non-sexual at first, but looking back now, the pattern was always the same. A long time before the sexual play even began; he had managed to relieve me of lollies, Easter eggs, and anything else he desired

24

for himself. Then, when he thought my defences were down and I was relaxed because he was being so nice and I could see no cruelty in his behaviour, he would take from me what he wanted.

His cruelty would return once again, and he would be sadistic in his pleasure because he had gotten what he wanted from me. I would get angry and storm off, stomping my feet, to go tell my parents what he had done, whether punching me, taking something from me, or trying to inflict some sort of pain on me physically. They just did not care. TV was more interesting or they would be involved with work, which left him and me alone, unsupervised, and to our own devices for hours, which he could use for his own pleasure. This pattern of conduct was the foundation of the behaviours that slowly, over the years, started grooming me to do more and more to him or him to me. And then, like a flick of a switch, my brother would start treating me like shit and be cruel to me again, which would be the pattern of behaviour affecting my life for the next forty years.

One such memory comes to mind and now suspends me in time, wondering if this small act of showing me something he could do with his balls was meant to be the start of his sexual play with me. He lay on the bed (I have a vivid memory of the autumn-coloured bedspread on the single bed) and proudly showed me how he could shove his balls up into his groin area with ease. My brother asking me into his room to so proudly ask me to watch as he deposited his balls up into his groin area and make them disappear from his ball sack into his groin. The first time I looked, yes, it was a big deal; I had never seen that before. But awhile later, he persistently showed me again what he could do, whereas I was more interested in what I was doing rather than in him. He later showed me again what he could do, and again I showed little interest in it—big deal; I'd seen it before—and I ran off to do other things.

His mind must have gone into overdrive, thinking just how he could get what he wanted and his needs met by me, his little sister. He was likely pondering how to get his little sister, who was four grades lower in school than he was, to do as he pleased and make her do as he commanded. The realization of how innocent he made this appear but how sinister this one thing, this supposed innocent thing, was so devastating to me. It came flooding back to me vividly, as I had forgotten that this had even taken place. This small memory fragment that had been there for some forty years was brought to the surface to answer another question that had not been answered: how had this all started? It's strange to think that something so small and presumably insignificant back then was so quickly used as the beginnings of a horrible entrapment of prostitutional service for the next six years.

Back then, when comprehension of my inexperienced juvenile mind saw this seemingly silly little act with his eager persistence to show me what he could do, it was the needed snare to entrap me into forcibly meeting his needs. He showed me on more than one occasion, requesting more and more diligence from me, insisting that I look each time he showed me. On the fifth time, he asked me to touch his groin and his ball bag his questioning of his truthfulness that the task he was showing me had indeed been achieved. The magical series of words achieved his desired result. My tiny fingers were carefully employed and instructed to feel the small skin bag empty of its contents, and he was rewarded by my naive touch. Snap! The trap sprang shut. He had achieved what he wanted, and already his broken record of persistence achieved at getting his innocent little victim, me, to yield to his desired results. He had me fondling his sexual member for his pleasure, manoeuvring me into doing what he pleased, and I became his first victim of child sexual assault.

4
CHAPTER

After that first seductive act was achieved, he learned how to control me, to get me to do what he wanted me to do. But now my dream world had begun, and an innocent little girl had begun to make her appearance in my mind from time to time as I dreamed my night away. This innocent girl was sitting all alone on her bed in the darkened house in which she found herself. Once my brother had secured his first reward of my touching him in such an innocent way, he quickly focused on his next goal. He had already managed to break down one boundary that I was unaware even existed, and he was well on his way to breaking down another. His persistence had paid off, and now, with one goal under his belt, he was able to see how he could achieve another. He had managed to get me to touch his private parts of his body once already, so his persistence in getting me to do it again would soon be realized.

With persistence as his friend now in this pattern of nasty behaviour towards me, he knew that if he kept asking me eventually, he would break down my barriers enough to get me to do what he wanted. Enticing me into his room, he began to show me his penis on a regular basis. I wasn't interested, and I would leave his room. His excuses for showing me what he wanted to show me became increasingly more and more elaborate, and he was becoming crueller and making me think that he hated me, even as he persisted in finding excuses to show himself to me, persisted. My desire to get back into his good books for whatever I had done supposedly wrong was paramount to me, as I hated being shoved into this outer ring of segregation, away from the family. The desire to belong to the populous of any community is at the forefront most people on earth.

The rest of the family followed his suit of segregated behaviour, with my losing more ground against their favour as well, as the fabricated lies to punish me got more elaborate by him. I did not wish to be on the outs with him, my brother. Siblings are the first real friends you are supposed to have in this world, after all. So manipulating me into service was easy for him to achieve. He had no conscionable reason to be nice to me, for treating me cruelly had already been a personality staple for him. I had stood up to my brother and said no, and he had not been allowed to do as he pleased with me, his little sister, but previous history showed that he never got into trouble for any of this bad behaviour before, so why not break down the next barrier that stood in his way: his possessing what he wanted. I was still too strong, and my brother was unable to break down the boundary he had come against. This small barrier that I had—oblivious to me because I was so young and had no idea it was there—was enough to keep him at bay for a little longer. I would need to be cut down, subdued, and made pliable.

Next to come was his getting me to touch his penis. Don't forget that he had already managed to persuade me to touch his ball sack, so the challenge to go further must not have been too much for him. He had to figure out how to get his sister to touch that part of him that was really not allowed to be touched by her. My innocence at getting him to stop asking me to see this cleaver little act he was doing my reward by the answering of this request I was left vulnerable to his clutches. At the tender age of eight, I didn't realize that the persistent asking of my older brother would lead to such devastating effects on me. His only thought focused on how he could get me to do what he wanted me to do, manipulation of the finest level, premeditated seduction at play.

By now, with his manipulation of me starting to become more complex in his sexual play making with me, there were the unrelenting as the relenting requests to see how swollen his penis was and how stiff it was being requested of quiet frequently. He'd ask me to touch it and examine just how stiff it was so he had an excuse for me to have to see it and touch it. The dream state I found myself in was far more complex than just the little girl sitting on the bed. She had developed and had progressed, and the room in which she was captive was off to the right of the kitchen of this house, which she only ever visited in my dreams at night, where this small captive girl was, always trying to escape from her world and having the realization that she could not. She was learning to quietly sit on her bed in this room and behave in a manner that would not draw attention and lure people to take notice of her. She'd wait without complaint and just wait in this now waiting room, for her to be needed by him, her captor and him to appear.

The spider's enticement into his room to see his penis was asked on a regular basis, and he was clearly determined to achieve his goal. Finally, he managed to get me to touch it again, another boundary gone falling in silent obedience at his constant request of me to get me to do what he wanted me to do. He had achieved his goal of getting me to touch it to see how it felt. The small blood-engorged member was stiff and standing to attention and now requested to see how hard it was and how stiff it was. I hadn't realized just how this clever, enticing spider was weaving his web around me, poisoning me with his words and beginning to suck any goodness out of me.

The achievement of getting his sister to touch it—the thing he loved most in this world, which hung between his legs. The focus of this young man and the desiring of it to be touched. But alas, the reward of victory would not be viewed as reward enough for long, as now, with this under his belt; he could see further victories in his future. The now-subtle manipulation was working perfectly to his advantage, being nasty and then flicking the switch to being nice, drawing me in close to get his needs met. He'd push me away when he got this wall of resistance from me, which he did not like and was determined to break down. It was working perfectly for him and had been for years now, long before his desire for sexual play had even begun.

Only now was I having the realization that my husband had used this same tactic to manipulate me over the years. This pattern of behaviour, which seemed to control my entire life, was currently being seen in full clarity. His sinister plot began to come to light as far as how he fitted into this picture of my life, what my husband wanted from my treasure box of owned wealth in order to make his life better and my life worse. The familiar behaviour of sorts from my childhood, forever entrapped in disastrous relationships, I was to be attracted to, familiar to the seeking. The platform that I would base all my male partner relationships on was in this patterned grounding culture that I was brought up in.

This grounded behavioural pattern was of push and pull and of being nasty, segregating me when I protested, and then, when my defences had weakened, they would come in for the kill and take from my possession that which they had deemed as theirs. There was now the realization of the single cigarette butt my mother would find every morning outside the family home, her never discovering the real message behind this deceptive clue. There was the apparent flippant dismissal of acknowledgement of such plain evidence of this supposed debt to be paid and the innocence of the victim's payment to be made. The smell of smoke her waking up and the subtle demand of payment that my family had to make, reminding my father that such payment had not been compensated yet and he was gently being reminded of such payment still outstanding. With the real issue of this family and its measure, the pawns in this game of life on a world scale, my realization of the clues were there but scattered in a million pieces, supposedly never to be put together and understood, but they were!

Finally, with his now seemingly ease at getting me to touch his manhood, asking me to see how stiff it was, I was asked to play with this member more and more. Him figuring out the next excuse needed that would warrant me the reasoning to have to touch his swollen manhood trophy which was given him at birth. My hands were employed to stroke and play with this pillar until my hands ached. My protesting at him seductively manipulated away so he could get me to continue with the stroking of his trophy. He made sure to treat me somewhat nicely so he could coax me into getting me to do what he wanted. My fear that I would be treated badly and be once again pushed to the outer rims of this family was a constant reminder that if I would just be nice and play his game, I would stay in favour in this family, or so I naively thought. My dream girl had progressed to escaping from her room, which had no door, only a flimsy curtain hanging where a door should have been. The cold dark room off the kitchen was tethered from escape. She sneaked across the floor from her room and through this kitchen, stealthily making her way to the door at the end of the kitchen, the target of her pending desire to escape from this house. This constant subject matter of her escaping, of my now developing dream state at night, was relentless. But locked the key removed from the lock and the relentless turning of the doorknob, the now failure to bless her with the escaping from this place. There was the fear

31

that she would be found out and her captors would hear the turning of the lock. Breathing heavily, she grasped the doorknob in her little hand, and as it turned, the air left her body at the devastating realization that the door was locked and she was still trapped in this house, leaving her deflated. When I would wake, the covers of my bed were often rather messy, as the obvious restless sleep pattern had again disturbed my sleeping body; the tormented sleeping pattern was obvious. There were now-regular attempts to get me to give him handjobs. The constant coaching of my work had begun the obedience required of the suggestions he now requested I obey as to how I could make this pleasurable experience for my brother better and more satisfying for him. As my tiny hands were manipulated into service for pleasing his member, my slavery chains, chained to this act, were complete now. The suggestion of my spitting on my hands was the next subtle request made, and his impatience was obvious as he gapped my hand. Saliva spilled from his mouth into the palm of my right hand, and as the clear white bubbles of the saliva dropped from his mouth and the strings of saliva tethered it until they snapped, it signalled that this next level of seductive manipulated behaviour was to begin.

Soon an occurrence for which I would forever be employed and so would my hands. My tiny hands were instructed repeatedly how to give him a handjob that would satisfy his need for lust fulfilled. He would instruct me on how something was well worth repeating or inform me that another movement was not pleasurable at all, urging me to either find a way to improve it or stop doing it altogether. He was making use of my mind, which was now engaged into the service of thinking how I could make this experience better for him so he would be happy with my effort for the day. My saliva rather than his became the desired lubricant on my hands, and I was required to spit on my own hands now, again more of me required in service to him as I was made manipulate the blood-engorged fleshy member of my brother's trophy. The sickening thought of this enslavement I was forced to do. Neither of my parents cared what was happening to me at the time, their pursuit of money far more important to them than the abuse that was happening to me under their roof.

As my little fingers began to develop their own style, more and more was required of me for his pleasure. There was the constant instructing of hand movements and how they could improve the experience for him now that I was employed as this being my job, was expected. Soon both hands would be employed, one on his member and the other carefully told to caress his ball sack, the persistent desiring of where this all began. I was told to handle this area carefully, for roughness would not be tolerated in this delicate area. As boredom soon set in on my part, the contorting of my body ached, for I was required to give more and more of my time and effort into this act of pleasuring my brother. The chains of slavery demanded a lot for a young girl of nine. I began to learn that roughness in the ball sack area soon meant I could go and return to my life, away from this torture. I would be punched or pinched, the reward for being rough with this delicate little area of his.

Now that a regular pattern had been established of my being in slave chains to this person, my brother, to fondle his manhood, miraculously, like magic, a double bed appeared in my brother's room. A large fuss was made of the new bed that was now in my parents' room, with the focus on the beautiful new bedroom suite that was purchased and how nice it looked in there. Little focus was made of the double bed conveniently deposited into my brother's room, which was adjacent to mine. The two small single beds were taken out of my brother's room and this nice roomy large double bed moved into place very timely, signalling what was to come next, signalling the acceptable approval of what he was doing to me.

After a while, this playing with his manhood (the pubic hair developing and growing thicker), the repeated handjobs were no longer able to hold his attention, even though my persistent development of new ways to stimulate him were employed. The constant requests to place my mouth over his member were now being voiced, with another boundary shaking under the weight of constant criticism that I was not achieving the required target of desire. He forcibly made me responsible for his pleasure and made sure I reached it, the current focus of his attention. How far could he push me to make me do as he pleased for the desired result of pleasing his shallow manhood? I was pushed away and crushed, and beatings were exchanged. I was then put into isolation and was told that my attitude needed to change. "If you would only work together … Why are you being so bad? Your attitude needs to change." And I would be made to feel bad, as though I had done something wrong for not wishing to do this next thing requested!

Pushed into isolation, I was criticized because my resolve to not do something that was asked of me was strong and I denied bending to his request. I had put up my defence, and that was just not acceptable. "Well, your attitude needs to change, young lady." That attitude was my having the audacity to protest that I was not going to do something asked of me. "Well, you will be treated so badly and crucified until that attitude changes because you need to behave in ways we want you to behave. You are being bad right now, and well your attitude needs to change. Work together, work together. Why are you fighting this all the time? You need to change your attitude. I don't want to know about it, and you will stay isolated and alone until your attitude changes. Go clean up your brothel. We will keep you in isolation until you find a way to change."

5
CHAPTER

The now-vivid memory of stuffing chocolate into my mouth was the earliest recollection of using a substance to quell the discomfort of pain developing in my body and the forbidden escaping of such horrors as the shame came to rest on my shoulders. This substance used to change my mood and stop the physical pain that dwelled deep in my body. I'd steal money from my mother's purse and walk to the shop just down the corner to get chocolate, stuffing it in my mouth and feeling the choc wafers melting in my mouth. As I type these words, I am eating the exact chocolate today that I ate back then, still using the same substance to quell the rising tears in my body. I'm barely able to eat three bars of it now, but back then, I devoured ten whole packets in one day. I stuffed the morsels into my mouth, the desired drug of a nine-year-old trying anything to keep the raging anger at bay.

One of my most vivid memories now is a repetitious one that makes this experience so strong, affecting me to so not just one time but also a multitude of experiences which make up this memory and still affects me to this day, and that was being forced to give my brother head jobs. His next step in exploiting his power over me was his constant request for me to lick and touch his penis with my mouth. Every time I was employed to keep the peace and stay in his good books of favour by doing handjobs, I was also asked to lick and touch his trophy with my mouth. I still find it hard to hold anything in my mouth to this day, as I instantly feel I am going to choke. I get a sore feeling in the back of my throat whenever I forget for the slightest moment and hold anything between my lips, until I am brought back to stark reality. It's such a maddening reminder of the years of being forced to pleasure his member.

I have a cell memory reminder of his fingers digging into my tiny scalp and almost pulling my hair as it knotted at the back of my head while he pushed my head down over him repeatedly. The prison entrapment of this servitude chains binding me, to this thought already years in the making and now stuck forever in my mind. There was smell of him, the odour of him while my eyes were either fixed on the sporadic pieces of pubic hair that were starting to develop or I closed my eyes until I protested and left his room after he unlocked the only internal door in the house that had a lock—funny that! It's an echoing reminder of the girl in my dreams and the door that could not be unlocked, similar to my dream world and the world that existed, suspended in time.

My forced obedience required more and more as his demanding servitude began to request more unrelentingly. Soon the use of my hand no longer satisfied him, and the use of my mouth was a now-constant requirement as these forced slavery attempts at pleasing him took over my life. He then demanded that I not use only my hands or mouth but now combine the two, the now requirement of my servitude act. My being crouched over his groin, my back ached in my silent protested displeasure, with the only view being his cock with this pubic hair. My desire to keep in favour so I would not be treated cruelly was the reason behind my obedience. The repugnant smell of his groin is still held in my cells, as are the memories of all I was forced to do. I will never forget the back of my throat being sore and my aching jaw required to stay open to maul this male member with my mouth, my hands also aching. I was reminded constantly that I was not doing it right and that if I would only do it his way, then things would be easier and nicer for *him*. The demand of this sexual abuser on his victim in order for him to obtain pleasure was the real enslavement of me.

By now, there was the constant preaching of my father to "work together," when regarding my hatred towards my brother, and his flippant "Don't give a shit about how you're treated," a reminder of what was expected of me towards my brother. The anger was building, but I had nowhere to put it or voice it, as I was not allowed to. Trying to subdue this rising resentment infecting my self-esteem was hard. I tried to make the experience less of a chore for me, trying to find a way to endure what I was being forced to do, but my ability to stop this process was long gone, as I was tied to this conveyor belt of moral destruction. Still, my mind tried to find ways to alleviate the pain it was forced to endure constantly. My family life was deteriorating into a lonely life of being yelled at that I had done something else wrong, as the pressures of business had become more of a reality. The responsibility of a family became more like a sentence for my parents rather than a joy. The more the abuse escalated, the more I was pushed out of this family and into the outer realms of family existence. The separation zone began to widen, and my family life became more like a battle zone than a soft place to fall.

As this act of pleasuring my brother developed, and the skill at which I was forced to each time to exceed the previous attempt, for his pleasure demanded more and more time, my anger growing. The self-esteem of sorts that I had left was now a constant effort to try to stand up slowly, only to be knocked down, forging in me a desire for something much better. When my brother had again forced me into another sexual act and his next reward was not achieved, he would start the process of being cruel to me and treating me like shit, pushing me away now, to isolation complete, leaving me wondering if I could return to this family circle of supposed love, that I was again sweet and accepted into "this family."

I was licking my wounds in my special place and me in the outer world trying to get in, all because of a horny teenager and his desire for his male ego to be touched. My parents would follow suit, and I would thus be treated with such disrespect for the next few weeks, as though I had done something wrong. I was banished to my corner of my universe until my attitude had changed. The manipulations of my world almost complete, the push and pull of this world the rubber banding of my feet. The ground that I stood was an ever-moving cascade of up and down expectations, never moving or changing. I'm over here, now my separation complete; I'm no longer apart of this family, complete. My wish was to meet my hopefully adoptive parents, who at some point must have been looking for me. I had developed the thinking that the only reason I could fathom at that age for my treatment was that I must have been adopted. How could parents deliberately allow such treatment of their daughter, their oven flesh and blood? Adoption must be the reason that these people I am with have no heart connection with me and thus find it natural to allow their son the privilege of sexually exploiting this girl his supposed sister. This seemed a logical explanation for me. Had they known my true parents just what types of parents they had left me with. Would they be shocked enough to rescue me from this hell?

After a while, my protesting at giving my brother so much attention became so anger driven that he needed to find something to keep me involved in the art of his sexual experimental desires and sexual exploitation of me. Thus he began requesting to see my private parts, oh so subtly at first and then more and more, requesting was done until again that boundary that was mine was now walked over also. It was snapped and broken, taken control of as though it were not there, and subdued into allowing my brother the privileged ability to take possession of the special part of my body that was supposed to be mine. The constant request to see this part of me was so relentless and my self-esteem boundary so flimsy that it too fell under the weight of endless knocking. My body had finally been conquered, and he now had me where he wanted me. His twisted, perverted requesting had paid off, and he had finally been able to say enough words and break down enough barriers over the years to be able to finally get to play with my not-so-private area at last. The length of time was considerable, and he held more and more of my lifetime in his hands. My ability to escape into my fantasy world had begun, as I was getting no relief from my parents in the way of protection from them, and my capture for my brother's use was complete. He owned me and controlled me and decided just how I should be treated in this family.

He began to fiddle with my vagina now with his fingers, at first trying to see if he could get me aroused. He'd lick his fingers to wet them before beginning to touch the tiny parts of my forbidden fruit with his wet digits. Because of his constant betrayal, our relationship as brother and sister was no longer recognizable, husbandly acts demanded. Each time he was asking me to do something else, to force down another boundary of my bodily defence that I did not know even existed. The protection for me to help me make a good match later on in life was wrecked and flimsy to the touch. The requirements for my platform on which to build my life and relationship structure were so damaged and mangled, the proper pieces all gone and destroyed. They were no longer strong and in place to protect me from unscrupulous men forging ahead in their desire to exploit me for their own desires. Gone and destroyed was this special wall of protection barriers given me at birth and required to be enforced by my family. Instead, I was being exploited and forced to relinquish all these precious barriers that should be there to protect me in the big bad world of unscrupulous men.

Therefore, I began pushing people away so they did not hurt me as my family did. I no longer had a healthy concept of who was naughty or who was nice, as sleazy men of questionable desires began to visit our home. Two years had passed, and the exploitation of my body was tedious. I was careful not to trust people, especially when it came to my body. I was already scared of what was going to be desired by other men, and thus my body temple became an impenetrable fortress of cold dead cut off. Separating that part of me off as if it were no longer mine, his manipulation of such precision and skill that I was made to behave at his will. I began to realize that I was better off not sharing my body with anyone and was trying to steal back from him something that was mine, and that was my body and control of who had use of it in the future.

I complained when, during one of his fingering expeditions, he would cut me with his nail and I would be left hurting. This tiny cut was so painful, and it stung as the body fluids and saliva would rush into this place and sting and pain. He would obligingly chew that nail off and quickly slipped his nail into his mouth in his willingness to continue touching me and not irritate me too much so he could continue to do what he wanted to me. Because of this, he would make me very sore, as urinating would be quite tedious after that and sting me as the hot acidic fluid would help to inflame this area more. It was very painful and another thing that I had to endure long after he was finished with his playing with me. Every time I went to the toilet, the stinging was a remainder of what he had done to me each and every time. I am not sure whether this was when I began my self-mutilation or not. I recall my first counsellor asking me if I self-mutilated, and at the time I said no, assuring him I didn't, as I was only focused on burning cigarettes into flesh and hair pulling and skin picking, cutting of the skin, chewing nails, to name a few, but after a while, I realized I was. But this would not be realized until long after my counselling sessions with him had passed and I was a distant memory in his vast career.

The girl of my nightly dreams was found regularly sitting on her bed sobbing. Upon waking, I would have tears streaming down my face. The young girl was trapped and all alone, with nowhere to run and hide or escape. The formidable figure, the enslaver, would come and shake his head at her as the tiny hand of the girl gripped the kitchen doorknob in the hope that one day the door would be left open and she could escape this world of terror. In this world where I was now so trapped and alone, the formidable figure was getting stronger and stronger, while I was losing my strength and getting weaker and weaker as the years progressed. The small unkempt girl of my dreams was visiting me more and more each week in my sleep as the abuse of me progressed. My parents' blind eye fully possessed the world I lived in, and I became as isolated as the little girl who lived in the home in that isolated wilderness of my dreams.

The fingering of my not-so-private body parts was of such that it was more painful after the act was over. My needing to go to the toilet was a constant fear, as the pain with urinating left me sore for days. When the torture of servitude was over, his nails cutting the tiny fleshy parts of the delicate part of my body was a constant reminder of what had happened to me, when the torcher of servitude was over. His constant trying to please me so he could continue his work on me was a priority. My protesting constantly that his nails dug in to me was in hopes that he would stop; however, he didn't. His stopping periodically to chew off a long nail so he could continue his assault of me was now commonplace. He had eager determination as he quickly flung his nail into his mouth and focused on chewing away that part of the nail that had cut me. I can still see his eager eyes staring up at my defiant body, seeing if his nail was still hurting me. He'd unlock the door, and I would be allowed to leave. I would go devour a block of chocolate in the hopes of keeping the anger and tears at bay.

My ability to find the words to protect myself was useless, as I had no defence mechanism available for my use. I was prohibited to use any verbal or physical attacks. I felt defenceless, and being protected by my so-called parents was non-existent. Again, my parents did not care. I had long ago learned that it was useless bringing my complaints to their doorstep for help. I had been abandoned by them, the door slammed shut on many occasions. However, if at times I did find the voice to yell angrily, my father would calmly take control of the situation and make sure to manipulate the conversation, making the complaint out to be of little concern, saying that I was making a big deal out of something of little consequence. The subject matter would be changed and lost into something that was less challenging to his conscience, no longer resembling the subject matter I had approached them about.

The ready supply of chocolate was in the fridge at all times, and I never once got into trouble for eating chocolate, even when block after block was stolen from the fridge in an attempt to quell the storm of confusion and anger building I was holding in my body. My large frame beginning to grow as a protection from males was a concern, as the forced containment of this angry energy caused me to supress more and more confused behaviours as though wrong were right. My battered body was weighed down from guilt made mine by the disregard of my protection from a father of equal disrepute. My boundaries were non-existent and my self-esteem lower, my schooling a trail of missed opportunities to comprehend. I was hollow and so unloved by the world around me and had nowhere to escape.

I just had to suffer the humiliation of building resentment, the downward spiral I was made to endure all because I touched his ball sack because he would not give up in his asking that of me. And then there was my father, who was determined to make this behaviour seem normal, at least in his eyes. If his son also behaved in this way, then his behaviour when he was young must have been normal; thus that was OK.

6

CHAPTER

Hindsight is an interesting thing! As a child, you are oblivious of so many things or, in my case, kept segregated so the whole truth and absolutely not the truth would ever be found out. As an eleven-year-old, keeping my world in control when coping with rampant child sexual abuse was a struggle. By now, comprehension at school was a joke. As year six rolled around, I was a problem in the classroom for my teacher than they liked. The solution, to avoid the "real issue" of what the problem was, was to become the focus of the next year. Being matched off to be evaluated to be sure there was not something physically wrong in my mind, perhaps the reasoning for why my behaviour was so bad. I mean my parents had to be seen to be at least trying to figure out why their daughter was so troubled, even if it was only so the outside world could be shown the trouble they were going to, to solve this problem they were having with me. The forced anger, unable to be contained in my small body, was beginning to escape. The floggings—the method used to keep me in control—were getting out of hand.

There were electrodes, charts, and meetings, and all the while, both parents knew just why things were so wrong but placed all the focus on me and my inability to cope with life, there must be something mentally wrong with her. Things calmed down for a while as the focus of better behaviour was expected in the classroom. Parenting skills were polished up, and we were on show, making sure there was not a hair out of place so they couldn't be considered responsible, as they were good parents. Years later, I requested to see the reports of this time to see just what was truly said, as the truth was all distorted to make me out to have *all* the problems in relation to this unruly behaviour being displayed. Poor parenting skill was the verdict but as an eleven year old that was not what was made out on the inside of 'this family'.

I regret not scrawling "child sexual abuse victim" across the chart, as I was still wearing this cloak of responsibility. This coincided with my discovering the self-mutilation that I was doing to myself. I'd been completely oblivious to the fact that it was even occurring to me. Refusing to admit that it was occurring on a much more regular basis than I felt I could cope with admitting at that time to myself.

By now, the ritual of handjobs and head jobs and fingering me no longer satisfied this advanced teenage man. My teens were not a reality for me yet, and I was to relinquish more and more of my boundary defence and time. His control of my soul was complete as he manoeuvred me into position to get his needs met—the chance stolen, that look, and more forced experiences to cope with. I can still see his expression, the quick glance meaning "What's next"—not asked but just forced upon, another thing to have to suppress. There was no longer the subtle suggesting persuading me into service. I was just subjected, just expected, and now forced to have to forget, to have to try to adapt to what was coming next. Then there was his look of getting away with it, my defence barriers no more met, because the barriers were just trampled when met.

He licked my vagina, the quick glace to see if I would

complain and protest at his next strategy. My response of protest was his expected reward for the small toolbox of protective skills all empty and all gone. He had the ability to force my defences to the ground, quickly and reliably, to groom me, to make me respond to his next idea what he was going to do to me. There was a pattern of pushing until he got his ability to groom me, to force me into his pliable subservience. The careful years it took to take his little sister from sibling to sexual slave were all done under the cloak of parental deniability.

This next grooming level was complex, with years of coached skills all in place so he got his needs met. The ritual of handjobs and head jobs was expected each time I was forced to come into this spider's web room of lies. In this next development, I was expected to put up with his face staring up at me from my not-so-private place. So oral sex consisted of my lying there while he stared up at me, in hopes of enticing me enough, wetting me enough, and sexually arousing me, with the hope that he would get whatever he was after, until I was allowed to leave. I can still see the almost look of desperation in the eyes of a young man with his face pressed to my vagina, the insides of the lower lids exposed because of his cheeks being pulled down and me numb and uncomfortable at being forced into having this done to me. This man, my brother, who was staring up at me from my vagina, was incredibly selfish, to say the least.

He tried in vain, as I forced my body to stand still and remain unstimulated at the command she made of my body. I refused to allow his constant stimulation of this part of my body with his tongue, to affect me. I had naturally now separated the sexual organs off from the rest of my body in order to cope with the manipulation of this bodily hole. I kept myself from noticing all the excruciating pain. The red roar of flesh was now constant and painful—no wonders I was messed up—yet it was to be considered quite normal behaviour for a brother to be allowed to do this to his sister. Not for one minutes did he think of anyone else but himself and his needs being met. In so many ways, these men cripple the essence of a woman for all men and sabotage the whole natural existence for future generations to come. People wonder why the world at large is getting worse not better, well may be this is a great place to start and realise just how selfish these people are to mankind.

By now, primary school was over, and I moved into high school with some relief, as my brother had finished school and I thankfully did not have to see the cunt at high school. At least at school, I had some reprieve from the continuous torture that I regularly endured at home. However, other things were happening at school now due to my now vibrating on such a different level from the other children at school. Their experience of such matters was still years away from their comprehension. Some coping behaviours had started to emerge from under the weight of enduring all this guilt and shame, creating resentment of my situation while continuously being made to feel there was something incredibly wrong with me. The focused reason for why I was being treated this way was my wrong attitude to this situation. So I started to employ behaviours that would mimic what was happening to me when I was treated nicely in this family. The only way to have "that feeling" now, that I belonged to this family, was to try to rescue the self-esteem that I had left from falling further into the abyss of segregation and total destruction.

In my dreaming world, another girl now joined me, as we both shared the same fate in this home. He had captured two of us as prisoners of this madman of my dreams. The collective vibration of family thought picked up in my dreams revealed another clue that would not be exposed until four decades in the future. The secrets withheld in a family collective were manoeuvred and hidden, concealed from sight. The ability to discover all was taken from sight and cast upon the watery abyss of lies and slights, the lock of this chest bolted tightly, with the key supposedly buried and out of sight. But messages revealed the buried truth as the universe exposed the timely truth.

The flimsy curtain that covered my doorway to this room was gone, and just an open doorway stared out to the kitchen on the left of her room of my dreams. During this time, her captive had become so cocky and reassured that she found unlocking the kitchen door and gaining my freedom in my nightly attempts was now easy. He stopped locking the door to this prison house, which gave her a sense that my escape was now close, that I could escape from this hellhole of horrors, the false wrongs would be made wrong not right. On the other side of this door was a whole other story. The two of them were still trapped in this hellhole of fucked-up moral glory. My captive's compass of moral soundness was no longer pointing true north but spinning uncontrollably in any direction, his concept of right was totally now gone.

It takes time to stop punishing yourself. You're not only the victim of someone else's sick obsession and cruel behaviour as the sexual abuse escalates but also now the judge, jury, and prosecutor of yourself in the committal hearing of your life and what you had to do to cope in a family who did not give a fuck about you. People were forcing you to change what was wrong into right, while they viewed you as just a commodity. So it takes years to stop being nasty to yourself and stop persecuting yourself for having this done to you and forcibly allowing this person to do this to you. But let's face it—you're younger and less experienced than the perpetrator, and you allegedly started this, enticing this much older person to do this to you. My heart physically aches at the thought of even trying to talk myself into that way of thinking now, as this is what the family and perpetrator try to get you to believe—this way of thinking. It gets the cowardly bastards off the hook if they can make you think you enticed him into doing this to you and there must be something really wrong with you.

So over many years, you are persuaded into thinking that you must be a bad person, for this is all you heard while growing up. The forced separation leaves you physically segregated from this family over there, away from them, so you are only able to conclude that you must be the problem here, while the other members of this family are all huddled together and supporting each other. Therefore, they must be right in their behaviour and mine must be wrong, and thus they stay away from me and no longer include me in this inner circle of knowing anything in this family. Over time, they slowly teach you how to take over the punishment of yourself that they have been inflicting on you. So the self-imposed punishment that you have conveniently taken control of keeps you in the position of victim and thinking this was all you deserved and this was your entire fault to start with. You've made your bed, now you lie in it. There's year after year of falling further and further into the abyss of self-destruction as more and more of life's shit is piled upon you because others from the outside world try to take advantage of this walking corpse of a person you have become, with no way of defending yourself because all your boundaries that you should have had were destroyed from the sexual abuse.

I remember coming out of a trance while sitting on the toilet. I think I was about twenty-eight years old. I found that I had rubbed my vagina so hard with toilet paper that I had made it red and raw. It took a few days to heal from this, and the only rational explanation was that I was replicating what had happened to me repeatedly when I was very young. It was after that that my self-mutilation took a different turn of events and I began to pull that apart and discover how often I had been mutilating myself. It's amazing how you can be doing something and not even realizes it at all, as the ability to trigger leaving your body, decades of forced practise under your belt, curse is broken, and you are brought back into stark realization as you re-enter your body. The years of coping by leaving the conscious mind and retreating to your now imposed jail cell of escape within the confines of your mind is so well practised that you are not even aware that it happens.

Up until then, I was not even aware that I had been doing anything like that to myself, and I suspect it had been going on for many, many years. I recall vividly when my first cherished counsellor asked me at twenty-two years of age about self-mutilation; I reassured him that I was not punishing my body. The awareness was not even comprehensible to me at that time. More often than I would like to admit, I would find myself coming out of this trance and doing it more and more as the insecure inner child struggled to recreate the feeling of belonging, to feel normal, all too overwhelming to a single mum of four children, in a marriage of someone else's convenience. I didn't even realize that it was happening until I would snap out of it, toilet paper in hand and feeling that familiar stinging sensation I received when my sexual molesting brother had fingered me so much that it stung. After about ten years, I managed to retrain myself to snap out of it quickly and not do it to myself anymore. The all too familiar punishment supposed loving behaviour mirrored in this act of self-betrayal.

During this period, I was able to piece together what had triggered it and why this feeling was so powerful, compelling me to be so cruel to my body. I attribute the trigger for this self-mutilation to my brother and his finger fiddling with my vagina at the age of ten. I can vaguely recall that I was doing this behaviour while I also lived at home with my parents, where this coping skill of sorts had begun, and as I said, it was many years before I stopped completely. The complete relinquishing of the soul so I could be controlled even long after my molesting by this person was over. His physical fingers at the control had ceased, and the years of abuse now matched by behaviours employed to get "that feeling" of what I was trained to think was normal took over.

By now, my self-esteem was even lower and the escape into my fantasy world was complete. Hours spent focused on my art work and craft allowed me freedom from my mind for a while. Throwing myself into a singular sport also helped in to use up some of this unexpressed anger and gave me a little joy in my life. Using these mediums as a platform to get awards for my hard work, this would be seen and bring praise for my parents and a small amount of positive attention towards me. The already emerging mental coping skills developed in order to cope with this heavy burden placed on my young shoulders. My overeating was taking over to stuff down those forbidden angry explosions and prevent them from escaping and forcing control over a lifestyle so out of contrast to what should be normal. My head was beginning to spin. The mental corrosion of my mind was continuously forced to edit the truth into lies. Still, that isolation was my only compensation, as the escalating dream world from which escaping was no more.

Now with so much complexity of the abuse that consisted of handjobs and head jobs, with my spitting on my hands and being continuously fingered until it hurt, was now somewhat soothed by his licking me out. The wet saliva of his tongue cooled the stinging of the previous fingering and soothed the pain being inflicted on me. The puppy eyes of expectations stared up at me, hoping that he would make me wet enough to have other pleasures bestowed. I'm escaping, I'm escaping I'm not even there. I'd somewhat mastered escaping from there. I was being used more regularly to get his needs, and I was very lonely, my world compressed. The control over my body at a master's degree as the rest of life was a complete tragedy. He was forcing me to stay and endure this assault, and I had little control over anything except my choc malt. But still I kept forcing my body to not respond, no matter how hard this bastard tried in this latest plot. To get me to squeeze every last drop, my personality sucked till it dropped.

For months, he tried in vain to arouse me, while the whole time I was forcing my body not to respond, the sheer hatred of this torture. It was my only defence I had left at my disposal against this person. I was again pushed away, and the isolation that I had become accustomed to, now my separation from this family, was a regular occurrence. I was trying so desperately to become a part of this family again and stop the torture of segregation away from this family pack. Why, oh why, was I on the outer perimeter again? What had I done? He was setting me up for the next level of degradation. He was about to manipulate and coerce me into believing that I warranted this behaviour, that this was all deserved.

Pushed away, unloved and all alone, I was out here with the wall of separation going up so quickly. There was no door. The wall separating me from this family was so tall and there was no end to what I must do to get through this very thick wall. I was all alone in this quarantine of life, my family all huddled and content and all right, with me alone on this side of their self-imposed wall, outside the fucking formidable family wall. Many of us who have been through sexual abuse have problems with our bodies, punishing them for being sexually abused, keeping them overweight. Trying to use this strategy as a protection from other unscrupulous people taking advantage of one's self. We are hard on our bodies physically in many ways, in a hope of trying to find that one thing that will redeem our souls from hell, finally allowing all the pain and anguish of a devastating life to escape. Freeing our souls from this hell and give us a balanced view on how we share our bodies with others.

My longing desire to be part of the whole, to be a part of this family so that I wasn't all alone, remained. I tried and tried in vain, though it was my constant desire to please and remain, belonging to these people. Why couldn't my real parents come rescue me from these people's claim? My survival was necessary. I was the only one I trusted in this hellhole of horrors, oh please why won't they come and take me away from this place. This constant desire used to control the small child in me, stunted me from growth in so many ways. The roller-coaster ride was now such a familiar patterned thing, the cycle of my life completely complete. There was no escaping, no running, nowhere to hide my imprisonment in this family, who was guilty in their pride. Money was more important than the comfort of me; I was now a victim of nonconformity. "If you would only change that attitude you have towards us and work together, maybe you will see that you will be allowed to be part of this families trust."

The confusion, the anger, and the unexpressed tears all piled up, all completely restrained, with my body being blamed. It was my entire fault. If only I would change my fucking attitude ... Yet I was left without instructions of how this could be done. I'm a problem, I'm a problem. That's all, this troubled girl heard, with no true solutions offered for this troubled girl's world. My sexual exploitation of this young body was almost complete, yet there was still more to come, the sexual abuse not yet complete. I was tired and strung out, with nowhere to hide. I was about thirteen when I received a different tide—just sink or swim, with no other choice made then something else to contend with another's guilt, party to shame I was treated so lame. Another boy to content his chance thankfully stolen, my body not violated, in his chance that was stolen. My world was getting smaller, with no way to defend myself and I mentally chose to put a lock on my sexuality so no other could pretend, while taking advantage of the scored land my experience had become.

Upon scrutinizing my fragments of memories that keep floating to the surface, I am reminded from time to time over the span of my childhood of the different ways I used to test the icy waters of truth in my family. I was not solely leaving the experience to fate but carefully watching for opportunities to alert my custodial parents as to what was happening to me and to save me from the situation that was obviously oblivious to them, or so I thought, while growing up. I understand at this point that you realize that they knew. They knew from early on what was happening to me but chose to obscure their eyes to it. I never did know they knew, until many years later when my mother revealed the truth to me about just how early on, they had known. My mother revealing a conversation with my father very early on when I was only nine that he knew but told her to shut her mouth as the scandal would wreak his business and that his money making was of far more importance than some female girl under his care.

I, however, had no realization that they were fully aware of just what was going on, and I was desperate to find a way to alert them! Desperation cloaks itself in funny disguises, and opportunities are searched for in many places in an attempt to alleviate the suffering you are subjected to. I mentioned before that I was positive that I must have been adopted into this family, as this would have made sense considering the horrible behaviour I was required to endure. I was not part of this family, so they didn't really have to care about me. Well, during the time I lived at home, I was subjected to many an opportunity to say something to my parents, not realizing that they knew what was going on.

The new girlfriend appears in my brother's life and was so lovely the focus of life once again was on him. I clearly remember the brush of my father's hand on her shoulder and the sharp disapproving look that she glares at him with. Her uncomfortable ness at his touching evident in her body language, as she flinched under his touch was so clear for me to see. Later my father's words the excuse given that she must have been sexually abused the reason for her reaction and not the fact that he had no right to touch her the way he had. Then reminding me of how graceful she behaved, even though he had made the assumption that she had been sexually abused also. Subtly being brainwashed over time that my behaviour was not acceptable but if you look at her whom also has been sexually abused you could take a leaf out of her book and behave like her. I was only told of the assumption that she had been sexually abused and I should behave like the young woman who started dating my brother. Again my father using an opportunity to program my thinking the way he wanted. My opportunity stolen again, as he change the subject matter quickly, so he had control of the flow of the conversation and thought controlled programming once again.

In hindsight, one such occasion which should have been talked about and fully addressed, but again that family piece of carpet was pulled and stretched, as its size was to increase, to allow another to hide his grubby mess. He was an old man when this happened to me, and had he any decency, he never would have done this to me. He was aware and in full possession of his faculties, but I was about thirteen and starting to see just the way it was for me. This anger energy was locked in the lower vertebra of my spine, the only place my body could hide the twisted emotions it was being forced to conceal the five years of enslavement I'd been made to endure already. My breasts were swollen from development, and shapely hips were starting to appear, womanly features starting to materialize and be noticed by others, especially men. It was a beautiful and special day. We had driven to visit family friends who were all very familiar to me. We were to retrieve a car body that would not be restored until some fifteen years later. But the opportunity had presented itself, so my father took advantage of the seemingly cheap car body of this early model Ford, which was available to him on the side of this shed so he could do it as a retirement project in the distant future.

These family friends were particular favourites of mine, as the elderly woman was practically an adoptive grandmother of mine while I was growing up. I would visit on a Sunday afternoon so I could chat and have company with someone I felt was the only person who loved me. I would ride the five kilometres round trip to their home and back to my house most weekends, using my pushbike until it was too destroyed for me to ride it. And these family friends had moved away to another town, and I no longer visited them, their house no longer just a few kilometres away from my own home.

After pleasantries were exchanged and lunch eaten, it was time came to go hunting and find that indeed this car body would suit his purposes for restoration. After parking and walking down the incline to where this battered car body lay, he ascertained its value, and promptly my father went back to get the car and trailer to retrieve the car body. While he was getting the car and trailer, which were not far up the incline, there was enough time for this elderly man of age to swoop in, grab my arm, and draw me in close. Pressing my body to his, he thus took possession of my body and fondled me for his own pleasure. I was taken aback that this man I had known since about seven would treat me in such a way. I was again subjected to a man who did not respect any boundaries of another person, one who was female, and he proceeded to grope at my breast as if he had a goddamn right of possession.

Scared and shocked, I stood back as the mistreated car body was winched onto the trailer. I got into the back seat of the car, my mind spinning, wondering how I could alert my father as to what had happened to me, now scared at how easy it had been for this man to take ownership of my body as though it were his to possess. We arrived back at the home of my family's friends, and I waited for an opportunity to bring up to my father what had happened. I was eagerly thinking that I would be redeemed and protected from such manhandling by his mate, a man I had known for many years now, which would thus lead to other opportunities to talk about other things. I broached the subject with caution and told my father what had happened before we left their friends' home so I wouldn't miss the opportunity. I was shocked at how fast and flippantly my parental guardian dismissed the incident as merely his friend seeing how I was developing, as if this, to my father, was acceptable behaviour for his friend to do this to his daughter. Again I was left powerless to control any advancement coming my way. I was totally vulnerable, with no protective claim made over me at all.

The next piece of meat on the slab to be fondled by anyone is this lovely girl of thirteen years of age. With low self-esteem and insecurity at this age, she is a vulnerable female available for your pleasure. Notice how the cute little boobs are starting to emerge under the blouse. Please feel free to come and squeeze the delicate fleshy parts of this walking carcass of meat, careful not to give a fucking care that you don't have this right. Just walk all over this female's boundaries as if they are not there, please. And yes, she is my daughter, but I don't give a fuck!

Obviously, I never mentioned anything to my father again, because I could see that if he was going to treat this with such little regard, then something of greater stature was also going to be treated in a like manner, and I was right. The congruency of words to action was just a smokescreen that blew away when any real test of true courage needed to be made. It was not his right to give consent to fondle me, which is what he had just done, like a gift on a silver tray. Worse, it was a family friend, old enough to have damn well known right from wrong. In addition, I was only thirteen years old and his daughter, even though this did not seem to hold any weight at all. What family values of any real substance did this family have and stand by? None of any quality that I could see, only the illusion of something skin deep, like movie set quality. It looks good on the outside but is propped by a facade, a mask held up for the world to see, to show that these people are of good quality.

7
CHAPTER

Over time, I learned to make the experience for me better so I could cope with it, not necessarily make it better for him, which in hindsight, it would have done, but self-preservation makes you very adept. You change what circumstances you can so you are a little more comfortable with the outcome of less pain, even though your heart is in turmoil and aching, your head spinning from guilt, for even at such a young age, this feels wrong. You're forced to bend your moral compass to accommodate his demands of you, and cruelness is dished out. If you don't, you lose a little piece of who you were and what you could have become. Over time, so you are more comfortable and not in pain physically you start to obediently pleasure him so you can somewhat have some control over what happens to you that day, even if merely not having to have his penis shoved so far down your throat that you choke. Kneeling beside him, your legs begin to ache and your lower back is in agony, so you contort your body into something that resembles forced pleasure.

Slowly, over time, you are being trained that a man's demands of you are far more important to him than any you should have or ask of him. You are trained to be walked over, stood on, and crushed, just plain trampled in male lust. This supposed head of the household was determined to crush any lasting self-respect out of me with his son's total control of my totality. I often wonder if my father saw me as a wild horse that needed breaking, the twangs of self-guilt imposing the hatred for his sister on me. It was the twisted thinking of a male whose sexual exploits of his sister now controlled the world in which his daughter lived. Saying that some old lady relative on seeing me said, I am determined and head strong bringing this supposed memory up when he was losing some fight, manipulating control back in its place. Saying that at my birth, it was seen that my personality could not be redeemed, that the disobedience was already seen, if it's really true or this is actually lies, my fate sealed by him for his conscious to rely, to program me that, that's the reason why?

By now, I was commanded to do whatever he wished of me. My ability to protect myself was gone, and I had no parents' authority to tell him this was wrong, that he should stop this. My parents were ever vigilantly checking my underwear for signs of my periods, making sure they did not have to explain any unwanted pregnancies. He was now trying to penetrate me with his cock, not forgetting I was only a little girl. My lying there was no help to his purpose, and I think it was the reason he did not succeed in his mission. Why would I know that you have to help guild a man into position? I was not aware that any help was needed in making his plans realized. He instructed me to lift my legs, but still I refused to give in and help in any way. I think he was getting frustrated with his efforts to control me as his plans were not realised. So pushed out the door and the process of running down my character again would be there. He was being nasty and hitting me, again pushing me to the other side of that family wall. My parents were being nasty because that's what they did until my attitude did the bending, the breaking, the sobering, making, my next solid boundary cracking their making.

This attitude meant that until they had crushed me and kept me so isolated, I would bend in submission and my brother could then manipulate me into doing what I was supposed to do. So again, when I had been treated with enough of their "loving behaviour" and my goddam attitude had changed, I would see that I was being treated nicer and allowed a token seat on the inner family circle for a while, until again I had disappointed them and was pushed back out to this outer wall— never realizing that coincided with my brother trying to break down another of my sexual boundaries so he could have his way with me. My changed attitude was a mixture of feeling so lonely because I was on the outer and trying to be good enough so I'd be treated nicer. I was also so crushed from defeat that I would slowly change my angry disposition into a less angry demeanour, all the time eating and stuffing my emotions down with food and chocolate, the supply restocked and easy to get. The recipes for my choc malt milk drink were becoming more elaborate the more I was abused; my afternoon feasts a king's morsel to be had as I stuffed the angry resentment down so as to keep the forced control of my emotions in tacked.

Sometimes this nice behaviour came early to me if we had a family thing, which meant they had to treat me with some respect and school me before the event to make sure that my behaviour was acceptable to the outside world, not angry, frustrated, and bitter. I was frustrated that I had no leg to stand on in this family for my defence and that anything I tried to stand up for got manipulated and shot down, quickly using words to turn what had happened into my fault rather than theirs. The angry fighting with my brother was a constant thing, and I was manipulated and unable to change anything. It was a waste of time now even to try, as all personal liberties that most take for granted were no longer mine. I felt like a puppet on a string, being pulled in every direction and made to dance how they deemed. My brother now controlled this family and how they treated me, having total control over each small facet of me. The trueness of me, my true personality, was fading further and further into obscurity as the essence of which I truly was falling deeper and deeper into my personal abyss of an unrecognizable plot.

Now in high school, things were somewhat worse but also better. I took the bus each day, as I had for the entirety of my schooling days, until the bus driver grabbed my hand when I went to put the money in his hand when I was about thirteen. He scared the shit out of me that day, and I'd never trusted him to start with, his sleazy demeanour eyeing your every move; I refused to take the bus anymore. Due to overcrowding, I had to change buses from the one I normally had taken, and my parents did not care. Because of the current government at the time and the recession, there was no pushbike for Christmas (few people had money, and interest rates were though the roof, with over 20 per cent interest rates for most home loans), and my brother had destroyed my last one. I walked to school from that day on. I never went on the bus again but walked the three kilometres to school and back again each day. This walking every day helped me to cope with things better, even though it was through necessity I was walking, but unbeknown to me, it helped with depression as the constant walking helped to quell the anger and help with endorphin release which is one of the brain chemicals for happiness and releases stress, which was quite bad due to forcibly turning wrong into right for six years and my soul breaking under the strain of all the family bullshit I was forced to hide.

Again I would be enticed into his room with this now-familiar treating me nicely and then making me do handjobs and head jobs, and now the fingering, the licking and wetting of his owned piece of me, until he would try to penetrate me. As I got older and my body got larger in size, the forced control over my body to make it not respond to what he was doing to me became harder. My determination however that I had to succeed and not give in to his demands became more complex and required more focus for me to achieve. Not responding to his stimulation of me vagina became my only defence left so I had some control over me and my body still. Unbeknown to me, my mental and emotional development had been held fast like in cement, for some time now. The ability to grow in these areas of my life, were long gone and the skill of growing maturity stolen and controlled. So to the outside world it may have appeared to look as if there was something wrong with me developmentally, as I behaved in a childish manner in some areas of my life. As my ability to comprehend just what to expect in my family home, on a daily basis now, my only focus to figure out a strategy, on how to survive that day. Other issues which would have been normal behaviour for a young lady my age just evaporated from my sphere of awareness. As now survival strategies were of more importance to me than any other trivial issues of the time.

Now, for some reason, he started covering his manhood with plastic, and I didn't really understand how all this made sense. This plastic device, which was just thin wrap, made me sore in a different way. I clearly remember the first time he jumped up and left his room running down the hall way into the kitchen and brought back the lunch bag he used first. Telling me that he would put this over is manhood so as not to make a mess. It had sharp edges and was placed in an area that had been played with and fingered and made sore. Weeks later he figured out that film wrap would be a better option to use. This plastic over his penis was just another fucked-up thing I had to endure and contend with, while not understanding just what it was all for. My family continued checking my underwear for signs of darkening discharge and all the tell-tale sign of my pending periods and womanhood. I was coming up on my fourteenth birthday, and the year had almost ended, with another to begin.

With my self-esteem lower than ever and my body larger, I was being constantly berated over my overeating, now a constant subject to criticize. My sniffing and chewing of my nails, not to mention my nervous ticks, was now a constant bombardment for my parents, and they complained that I should be better: "Oh, why do you do these things to shame us? You're supposed to be perfect; why you don't conform? We have brought you up perfectly, but still you leave us forlorn." I find that even today when I am going through times of stress, I sometimes revert quickly to chewing my nails or another nervous strategy from my childhood returns. I find myself with my hands in my mouth and beginning to chew. It's difficult to stop, and I can be found doing this many times over the day. It is quite exhausting to force yourself to stop and focus on changing your behaviours. My ticks that I had creep in, and I just have to remind myself to be gentle and loving to myself, as these were all coping mechanisms employed by a little girl in a home where she had no other way to cope. And some people wonder why people who have been sexually abused take drugs. It's one of the only ways they may have found to use to help get them through the day and feel normal.

Being beaten, sexually abused, verbally abused, and mentally manipulated into servitude, the coping behaviours used against me, I was finding it hard to even live in this home where my supposed loving parents were treating me with such love that I should be goddam happy because I didn't deserve a damn thing. "You're such a problem," they said. My battered body from years of sexual abuse was just tired of fighting for my life. It was a constant battle of wrong made right. I was angry and frustrated at having no rights in this family of sorts. The young girl of my dreams, now so desperate to leave, was trying anything to find relief. My dream world was still making its nightly parade, my mind trying anything to get some life, stake its claim. Her hair was unkempt, her soul beaten down. When would this hell end?

When will she be allowed, to leave the house of horrors? Oh Christ, why didn't my true family rescue me from these bastards and save me?

The final stage of my sexual forced development no longer was my possession, this body of mine his sexual play toy for his sexual joys. The final enslavement of my body and soul was when he made his penetration in a different end. The abuse progressed from handjobs to my having to touch his penis for a while and then having to use my mouth; to being fingered; to having oral sex preformed on me by him; to trying to penetrate me, to no avail; to his trying anal sex on me as well, the final thing he tried. This is possibly the hardest thing to talk about now. I sit here with a two-litre container of freshly opened creamy light chocolate ice cream beside me. I am at a loss as to what to write, as this is such a demoralizing act to do to someone who does not have control of anything if they are having this done to them. I had no control over any of my boundaries at all.

They were controlled by someone else and owned by another. My thoughts are very low and in the darkest place, my emotions almost not existent, and much deflated I am actually finding it hard to breath, and my back aches where my kidneys sit. They say the kidneys hold the deepest of your secrets. I am just numb at the thought of the lengths I was forced to go to, pushed and contorted, the small helpless child made to commit acts of unspeakable destruction of character. Sercombe to having another and my bodily boundaries forcibly crumble, a precious final boundary, forever gone and destruction left in its place. If I had the choice myself, I would never personally have crossed this threshold, but this choice had been taken out of my hands of control, from the minute I was born. As this sexual exploitation was coming to its end, there was nothing at all left in his conquering end? I was beaten and crushed. He got what he wanted, to force himself into me, making sure he put his stain inside me to fully break and destroy that tiny little girl I was, no never his sister not ever was I. The possible onset of my emerging womanhood periods, my ever-so-vigilant parents checking my darkening discharge on my undies, the real reason my brother stopped exploiting my body for his sexual gratification, one thinks. Then there was the hideous realization once told me by my mother, that my parents were willing to allow my brother to get the utmost use of my body before he was made to quit his despicable play with me. How does one come to terms with being sexually exploited on a regular basis from such a young age?

I was at the tender age of not even fifteen, when some young girls on their own desire to begin exploring sex, and mine was not finally over. Now bound in my history, now etched on the slightly beating organ that was referred to as my heart, was this unbelievable experience that was the beginning platform on which I was to build my life. I had already been forcibly used and abused, disgraced as no more than trash, in more ways than just sexually by this age. I had been forced to experiencing sexual acts that even to this day and age; most will have not been subjected to or experienced. I wonder if the universal God sees and feels a young person's heart break in such a manner. Is it thunder to his ears or does he even shed a tear as the sexual exploitations of this first victim of this child molester person finally end? It's the twenty-first century, and still young people are being treated in this way, as though we hold no sacred value to the human race at all, except the sexual pleasure of the depraved. These people, whom vibrate at such a low level of conscious existence of the human race, still exist. Their frequency of human conscious thought, being of such low vibration level needed to be able to do this to another human being is thus hard to fathom.

That dark spoiled area of my life was never trampled on every again by anyone, and my feelings of that time are ones of utter shame. A bit of ice cream about now should do it. I recall saying to my first counsellor that in a way, my brother was the equivalent of my first husband. My counsellor, stunned at my statement, had to admit on reflection that that was actually true, shocked even though he was at the starkness of this reality, my evaluation of the situation. My brother crossed so many boundaries that never should have been so flippantly taken advantage of, with no regard of the consequences to my soul. There was no consent given and no understanding of what was being forced away from my ownership, with little regard that I owned the ownership of such boundaries or procession of these personal gifts. The ripping of said ownership was made without my consent and without my comprehension that they were of my sacred ownership. It was stolen before I could be old enough to take stock of just what was stolen from me, until many years later, on reflection. So in a way, I look at the pending police action as my divorce and settlement hearing—forty-three years too late.

CHAPTER 8

He saw an opportunity to have me crushed and my soul broken, without having to lift a finger, by allowing his son the responsibility to do the job, years later wiping his hands of any responsibility like the coward he was. I recall my daughter yelling at me in a car once about how dare I ask him to deal with this situation with my brother. Again my father was using another's energy and voice to get across what he wanted to say, this time his granddaughter, to fight his battles, too gutless himself to do it. So again I find myself questioning everything that had ever been told, scrutinizing every fragment under my solitary soul of the now-truthful verbalizing of anything told. Everything for comprehension now comes from such a different place than the once-pilloried preaching as my ears faced his face.

My sexual exploit was over, the physical body all battered and torn, all supressed, together all crumpled and protection pillars all gone. My new suit of clothing shame, distorted and sewn together by lies designed to make the hearer think the way they were programmed to think. The now-verbal battering that was to begin its onslaught none too late in its delivery. Hateful and nasty were the words used to distort ones character, all to shape the criminal's distort of the situation that they had created. My shoulders so broad were carrying the weight of the whole crime, which had been placed upon them, from the two prominent men of my family. My character did they wrought, but whom gives a shit it's only a mere female anyway. Just a set of holes to be exploited and she is no value really anyway, there is something wrong in the head with that one! Any accountability coming his way, the mud-slinging flung in my direction, claiming that I was a slut, my character smudged, and him standing tall, all the blame for his crime he was now making mine. A different dilemma was about to bequeathed like a sledgehammer to the heart; I was made just a tart, no more an upstanding girl but just a dirty little whore. This new road smelled bad, but he paved quickly to sell, no one to tell I was living this hell.

He had already been nasty to me for years before, so this was just another way he could be nasty to his sister, and sell his story as being the one that was true. It was the next step in his evolution of relationship with me. His parental consent of the incestuous behaviour was given, and he had pushed over every boundary I ever had procession of. I was completely exposed and vulnerable to the world. It pains my heart to reminisce of the relationships with my husbands and admit that my brother did more to me sexually than my two husbands combined; thankfully, they were much gentler and kinder than my brother's way, at least sexually. This was the platform I was left with to build my life on, shattered and with no conscionable boundaries left to defend me, just completely ravaged and exposed to the world as damaged goods to be exploited. I was advertised, as nothing more than a whore to any hearer of these words, as they were spewed in cocky delivery, for the world to hear.

As my now verbal abuse progressed, my self-esteem sank lower and lower, until the turning point of none. I was getting very little attention from my father or mother. I was empty and needy, with very little of my emotional, physical, and mental needs ever being met at all. My overeating issues started to become the constant subject of my parents. My grandmother would say things like, "I'll be as fat as a house one day if you keep eating." My family kept making me feel bad, but meanwhile my mother kept a ready supply of blocks of chocolate in the fridge, and they would disappear all the time. I could devour a block of chocolate quickly, leaving the wrapper wherever, under my bed, in the bin, or hidden somewhere else. I rarely got into trouble for eating the amount of chocolate I did. It's a wonder I do not have sugar diabetes, but I more than likely will when I'm older, which energetically diabetes means, life is not sweet. When they were gone, I would find that I would have a new supply of chocolate in the fridge that next afternoon.

It was here that I think the bragging of what my brother was doing to me started to be talked about, as other boys started to take a lively interest in me. Or maybe they could see the shell of a person I had become, unkempt and crushed, so they could take advantage of me easily, or so they thought. Another boy in the neighbourhood—of about sixteen, I guess—also wanted me to do things with him, but thankfully nothing much happened and was stopped by an incident that freaked him out and scared him off, so he never came back, thank God. The pending discovery of people hearing about the exposure of what he was trying to do was enough to evaporate his courage in trying to abuse me sexually also, fleeing and never to return, thank goodness, as the exploitation of me by one person was enough to handle at that time.

I was a shell of a person by the time I was about fourteen and a half years old. I was ravaged from years of abuse by now, my character stooping to almost asking my brother for attention because it was all I was getting of any sort. I was like a hungry puppy dog begging for a morsel, only to be kicked to the curb for even daring to ask. At fourteen and a half, the abuse stopped, and I would like to think it was me and my disgust at myself and my anger at this stage that made him stop, but my counsellors say they stop because they have all the control in these situations, while I had none. I dare say that the darkening mark in my undies was showing also; someone may have intervened to make him stop, but again I will never really know. I was getting to be quite a big girl by this stage, and my anger was starting to get increasingly verbal. I had even started to use my fist for the first time. I think he would have pushed his luck had it gone on any longer; I would have flattened him with my fists. But truthfully, I think it was the fact that he was getting his sexual need fulfilled by other girls in the neighbourhood who also had low self-esteem. They were easy targets for him to conquer and thus take advantage of, as this was now his pattern for many years now, just keep pushing until he got what he wanted. He was almost eighteen by then, and he had a licence and was able to widen his scope of territory to find another to play with his manhood.

From here, the abuse by my brother was not of a sexual nature at least, for it had finally stopped finally, but it was more of a verbal and decimating of character at this stage. The yelling out of a car full of his mates that I was a slut, tramp, whore or anything else would be hurled out of the window of a passing car as it sped by, which was extremely shattering to the soul. With self-esteem low and the verbal taunting of a young man intent on shaping my future the way he wanted it, I found it hard to hold my head up. My clothes were plain and drab, not flattering to my enlarged body so as not to attract attention. I held a fake smile on my face constantly to fool onlookers that my life was joyous, when in reality I was an empty shell of a shattered life, existing on a thread of nothingness. I hid behind the tortured eyes that existed in my skull and the thrashing of my soul eager, to escape the clutches of these barbaric bastards who had held me in an embrace of tightly controlled sexual pleasure for their son. I was shattered and numb, my carcass dragging itself around void of any real care, wishing to escape to be finally left alone and untouched my only real focus.

My now-shattered carcass was soon leaving school and being forced into the workforce to earn a living, still reeling from the abuse that was six years long and the Stockholm syndrome that had developed living in this home, my willingness to grow crushed and blocked years earlier, now pushed headlong into a world of others and too immature to understand life. I was waiting, held suspended, for the next spine-tingling abuse to start as the last seventy-two months of my life had been. There were two thousand two hundred days of life under the sexual control of this man who had manipulated my mind, soul, and body into doing what he wanted me to do for his pleasure. I was to just move from being an abused girl who was controlled by her brother sexually, to think and behave how he needed me to, to being a young lady who had a mind of her own and worked and held down a job, able to present herself to the world as a beautiful woman, confident and ready to find a suitable man to settle down with and build a future for herself. What a complete fucking joke!

Dumbstruck from so much being controlled and manipulated, I was now pushed out there and forced to live a concealed life, punishingly suspended from growth and expansion, numb and just barely able to breathe in this world and reeling from sheer shame and broken boundaries. I often hear people talk about what they wanted to become and the way they envisioned their wedding or how many children they expected to have and glimpses of what they held their life to be, while I was just trying to breathe and get though each day. The torment of mind was so rapaciously grinding my soul into the ground so that I longer had distraction from my tortured soul, the aching of what is normal, never able to even comprehend the word because I had lived a life of a sex worker, now retired at fifteen, with little or no schooling to save myself, pushed out into this world to look after myself and my needs. I no longer truly knew what those needs were because for years I had been trained to look after another's needs and totally forsake any of my own needs completely.

On the other side of the kitchen door, my dream world resumed. There were stairs that went down into a laneway, the carport, the little lean-to where the car was parked. It was always reversed to make departing easier, and there was a little white sedan there. The kitchen door was now always unlocked and open, and the car in this space was where she made her nightly attempts to escape. This car was now where all her focus was. She wanted to get in it and drive it away. There were frustrating attempts at trying to get in this car, the cold door handle in her small hand another barrier so hard to escape. If only she could create her escape and be carried away from this place. Her hope grew, and each time I would make a slight improvement, but the figure that stood there reinforced her dilemma. That figure just stood there looking down from the top step, in the now-illuminated doorway, just shaking his head. It was the familiar silhouette of a man whose hands held my fate, his head going from side to side, resembling the pendulum of my changing life. As the determination of the girl soon turned to anguish and tears, there was a smirk of self-gratification that he was in control. Her hands gripped the car door, wishing for it to open and maybe provide some protection. This smug figure was just smirking at her, for he knew I was his. I awoke with my heart pounding and my hand clenched and sore. I was no longer victorious in my dream world anymore.

Now I was left with another dilemma to have to protect myself from, as my molester was making damn sure all the young men in the town had the opinion that he wanted them to have. He would also promise me things, only to let me down, lie to me, and steal from me. It was a trait I now realize that my future partners had, but at the time, I was unable to figure that out, as just the familiarity of their personality treatment left me feeling somewhat secure because that's what I was used to, so I felt at home being abused. My family gave me things only to take them back again, as though they were still theirs or had authority over my possessions as well. Nothing seemed sacred and off limits to any of them. My parents did not care what he said to me. They said I probably deserved it, so I should shut up and put up with it, me with my stupid little bitch attitude, serves yourself right. So it did not matter how spiteful he was or how hurtful he was to me. I had no one to help me where he was concerned. He could do as he pleased, only now it was verbal and mental abuse, eager to give the impression that again it was me to blame here and definitely not him. A stamp was put on me that I was just plain bad news in the town, and it was hard to get out from under this constant abusive control.

It was about this time that the toll of my brother hurling verbal abuse at me from a passing car started to take shape. These occasions led to my being put into many a situation from which I was very much compromised and almost raped on more than one occasion. It was about then that one of his so-called friends took an interest in me. This friend of his was much older than he was at the time, and I had finally left school and was working, so I was about sixteen and a half. He tried hard to conquer me sexually, without luck. I was saved by another of his friends, telling me he was married. I stopped seeing him after that, and I think one of my friends took over with his sexual needs (thanks, Trisha—it took the pressure off me) while his wife was in the Brisbane hospital for back surgery, or so he said. He lied about everything else, so why not that also? She was probably giving birth to one of his babies, if the truth was known. I rang her and told her what he had been trying to do with me. I never spoke to him after that. My father blamed me for that, as though I had instigated it and pursued him, but this young man had pursued me. But again, why would my full-time guardian care; he was only interested in keeping his life smudge-free and having money coming in all the time so he could achieve his monetary goals.

Another such occasion was when my brother's best mate climbed through my bedroom window and I found him in my bedroom hitting me up for sex. My parents were away somewhere, and I was there with my brother, who had just moved out of the home. I tell you, I have learned to do some fast verbal talking to get myself out of situations I had been put into. So I managed to draw this young man into the lounge room away from the bed rooms. Where sitting there he placed his hands on my thighs and asked me to have sex with him. I felt panicked and scared. Again in a situation where from this point on I was unable to find the words or the skills to protect myself as all had been stolen from me in the past. Finally when he realised I was not going to take off my jeans and allow him to sleep with me did he leave.

Again, I was stopped at the side of the road by his mates and propositioned for sex late at night from the young man on my way home at night. When all that stands between you and him is your pushbike and the ability to sweet talks your goddam ass out of the situation, it's exhausting and scary. And then a so-called boyfriend telling you that he is not taking you home until we had sex, and you are curled up in a ball on the dark, cold floor of some strange house, wishing the sun would come up early so you can walk home does not really build self-esteem and trust as far as the male human race is concerned. There are many occasions to pick from, but I can thankfully say that I told them all to go jump and never slept with any of them.

From this experience, you learn a valuable life skill and that's an ability to adapt to any situation, no matter what it is, and finds some way to endure it, no matter what. You're also adept in your ability to find some good out of the most horrific things that have happened to you, finding that every cloud has a silver lining. This skill that I was forced to have to develop has come in very handy many times. Most people don't have staying ability, but someone who has been through this can endure a lot for a long time, longer than most. However, that's also a downfall because you stay too long and keep taking abuse when most would have left. The ability to adapt to any situation and make it beneficial for me is a skill that I value in my repertoire of skills that I learned from having to endure being forced to do sexual favours to my brother. I look at that as a positive after the bullshit I had to put up with. This life skill adaptation has helped me in life more than once, and I picked it up after having to adapt to being forced to give my brother his sexual supposed due, according to my parents, for more than six years.

Remember, every cloud has a silver lining, and this experience was no fucking different. It's just taken me a lot longer to find the blessings I got from such cruelty to me but from which I was able to draw from some blessing, so I won in the end, not him. So even though you have to adjust and learn to somewhat separate that part of you, you know that some part of you has to pretend to like this process so you can endure it. It's because of this that you have this skill. You compartmentalize your whole person. Your feelings, your memories, your body and its parts, your experience of the whole thing is put into another part of you that you don't allow anyone to find or touch, until you're pushed into the tiny part of you that is nothing of the child you could have become if this had never happened to you, the part that's still you, which he managed not to steal. So in a way, your whole life has been stolen from you, and now the process of rebuilding a life worth living is reconstructed out of this rubble that is left, which, believe me, is not much.

9
CHAPTER

A reptilian response of controlling do-to-you-as-we-please attitude towards me, walking over me to get what they wanted, with no payment made for the soul virtues stolen, just crushing me underfoot as if I had no value. The abuse over the years of living in a reptilian-type home made me limit the amount of people in my life. Physically you learn to pull back and constrict everything in your world anyway, for fear that outsiders will find out. Your essence, the sharing of your soul's spark of life, is all held in and restricted. There's the resultant hiding, the pulling back, the lack of sharing yourself with anyone else to protect and hide the timidness and the loneliness, which all takes its toll. But in your reality these people are normal because it's the only thing you know, so others must be the same. At some point, your inability to distinguish who are good and bad becomes so foggy because the people who should be good and loving towards you are so cruel. To them, you are a commodity crushed, destroyed incubators in which to cook up the next scheme that will be put into play when enough time has ticked by, how to get from you what they want. This affects how you judge people in your world. When people who are supposed to be friends cross you and harm you, you become so distrusting of the world that you keep everyone at arm's length so you can protect yourself from more harm.

Your only protection from these people is disallowing them into your world as much as possible, for you fear they will also walk all over you and do as they please, just as your family members did. The battle armour of boundaries was forcibly crushed and denigrated long ago, walked over and disregarded as no longer yours to enforce. The wall of self-loathing is so penetrable, and the one-person army has no resistance to conquer it. Should not these reptilian bastards be rejected forever for the blatant disrespect of another's personal body ownership or are they still going to be allowed to do as they please and exploit another's body as they soldier on, crushing the soul spirit of future generations to come in their attempt to control that which is so out of control, which is them? This demasculinized energy of males is no longer seen as a gentle strength of honour and integrity once held; it is now turned to lust and disgust as they conquer and maim, with no conscience of wrongdoing.

One significant thing that is so evident is the sheer anger that we now carry like a shield of protection. Being wronged as we have, we have a real hatred inside from being so betrayed and wronged but little voice to shout out in protest. I think it is warranted, but it's not really understood by the world, for they look at us with eyes of judgement. I carried with me a lot of anger, and physically it was shown outwardly as being loud and boisterous, fearing that I would once again be put into another situation where I would lose all my personal freedoms. I was angered by my inability to build a defence mechanism of boundaries, which may have given me some defence to the continuous onslaught of abuse received. I was continuously made to curve and quell anger because in this type of reptilian family, your anger about what is happening to you is definitely not allowed. While this is all happening to you, you cannot control the building anger and frustration at your lack of protection from your family. The premeditated seduction of my virtue was continually adjusting wrong into right and ended up being a life sentence, a burden I was forced to carry alone.

I was repeatedly counselled that my boisterous and angry demeanour would make the boys not like me and make people think I wasn't nice. So on the one hand, you have this battle inside where you are screaming and seething with anger at having this person take possession of your own body on a repeated basis, the control of which is no longer yours. Then, on the other hand, you try to portray that life is fabulous, that you are happy and being nice enough so the boys don't think you're an angry, horrible person. You live with the fact that you're being forced to do things to please your child molester, but on the other hand, you're not be allowed to voice any hatred towards him or anger towards the injustice that is placed in front of you to swallow, just as his cock was. In this family, another controls your rights. Your rage builds as they instruct you to behave in a way that will not give the outside world a cause to wonder why this young girl is so angry. What would the neighbours think?

My anger turned inwards, and the self-loathing grew, and I was berated and told that if only I would change my attitude, things would be so much better for me. The stress and anxiety of living in such a strange way was not yet comprehensible to me, and I didn't know just how really wrong all this was until many years later, when I could evaluate just what had happened and this type of stress began to subside. The countless ramifications of that time echoed through my life from the minute I opened my eyes. The scrambled mess of memories were all screwed up and thrown together along with whatever the latest drama in my life was, all designed to distract me so I would never figure out just what was going on. They were always being nasty to me, as was the custom. My brother and his countless revolting comments to me were all designed to shape the outlook that I was a slut and it was my fault that this was done to me. My nervous demeanour was commonplace, the fight still there but the battles not won. I would stand up only to be knocked down.

The young girl of my dreams was so defeated that she sank— the bottomless pit of her heart all but worn through, the bottom of her heart so thin—about to fall through and unable to find any comfort to renew. She was never relenting in her dream world to escape. Finally, the car door opened, but there was only the deafening whirring of the dead battery motor, going over and over. If only it would ignite. When would I get this spark of my desire to escape this hellhole, this home where I was placed, the figure standing in front of the car, her pathetic use of anger a waste of non-control, no protest march belonging in this place? Her defeated spirit slumped over the wheel, her hands gripped to that circling wheel going around and around. Was I ever going to be able to leave this place? My heart ached a deep soulful rhythm of years of relentless defeats as to why I bothered rising to my feet, the mournful despair of my heart beating that now I had no story written on my soul's future path, all scribbled there by others, their future my path. Being led like a donkey up a garden path, I was empty and crushed, with nothing left, just shattered to dust. I couldn't breathe now but must, although shattered from his lust.

My room was cold and empty, as if my heart, my soul, was so crushed and the slow beating rhythm of a girl was so destroyed but smiled now and behaved so no one would ever know or question what was wrong with thee.

"So put on that smile and sit up straight and don't chew your nails. Stop sniffling your nose and don't eat too much—your eyes are bigger than your belly—and stop watching telly. Look like a lady and a proper girl. You poor hard done by child, why are you so sad? If you would only change that attitude, you would be glad. Don't step out of line and make us look bad. You're supposed to be our daughter, not out of control. You're a problem, for Christ's sake just behave. You're not too old to flog. Don't forget that too—and I don't want to hear about how your life is just shit. We are not interested in what you have to say. So shut the fuck up and stay over there on the other side of that wall, where we don't have to look. Get away from me. You make me sick. You played with his prick. You're to blame for all of the shame you withstood.

"You've made your bed, now you lie in it. We have no shame. Shut the fuck up and keep a stiff upper lip. We don't want to hear about it, so cover it up and get out of my sight. You make me sick because you played with his prick. Stay over there; we want no part of you. We are more concerned about money to date. We don't give a shit about you. You're just here to berate. You're now just a hole for the next male to exploit you hard done by girl, aren't it time you grew up and faced that this is your lot in life? So don't expect any cake, because we will give you nothing, except more of the nothing to expect now as the norm. Go clean up your brothel, you little whore. Now we are programming you to survive."

After my schooling ended and I was at work, the dream world took on a different turn. My dream girl escaped the car door was unlocked, and my brother's cock was now soothed and stroked by some other brunette lock. I still lived at home, and the sexual abuse had stopped, but I still had very little rights of my own. His frequent visits afforded him control over me. There was the constant berating that I was a whore, my character no more. I was made filthy and loved not at all. He assigned my fate that I was nothing more than his discarded sexual playmate. I was a survivor now, or so I was told; I would survive this and be as good as gold. His hateful words were designed to place all the blame on me. He was beyond reproach, just ask me. He would claim that his upstanding son was the next pillar of this community.

I was dead inside, with nothing left, a walking corpse, and

the essences of life all gone, a shell of a person no longer whole. My existence was nothing more than a mere shadow of the girl whom was made to be a whore, drifting through life all shattered and torn. My existence was no more than a struggle of fighting to own what was no more than the title of a sexual plaything, disregarded and forlorn, my identity all gone. I had no idea about this girl that I was, a skeleton of holes to be exploited and shoved into a box sealed and locked from above and then stowed in the corner, labelled survivor for sure. The deep abyss of the heart that had fallen though the cavity of my soul, on which I was now expected to build the future foundation of my life, was just numb. The heart was barely beating now, for what use was this organ, just faintly beating with the essence of love for which I never received? This faint wisp of a loving heart was what I was supposed to go out into the world with and find someone who would love me. I am not a person who resembled any due, just the corpse of a person I dressed and tried to look new. The empty eyes stared out, not caring what happened. I just wanted out of this family's contraption.

The head of my household, who is the one to set the rules of a family, was so corrupt himself and would not do anything about it, and why should he? He would have to face his own demons. My dream girl was so crushed and desperate to leave, having the keys in her hand. As the key began to turn in the ignition and the motor came to life, the shock that it turned and actually fired up made my dream girl gasp and surprised her. Her foot jerking off the accelerator pedal made her stall the car. There was anticipation of escape and, a little further in the deluded reality, of some control over her life and her hopefully pending freedom. She sat there and started it again, and the realization that she could escape was a real possibility. I had started driving lessons and began to envision how I could find a way to leave this mess that I called family. My lessons were progressing, and for a while, I found that this small freedom of sorts left me thinking that I was free.

I was freer than I had been allowed to be for some time, and as I drove around the town, I could feel the growing anticipation that I would soon be able to have some freedom. But again it was like giving candy to a baby, only for it to be taken away. I was fooling myself that I would be treated with some decency, and I sure was not going to be allowed to drive the precious cars of my family, so again I was given a taste of freedom, only to hear that I really cannot drive anywhere. They wouldn't allow it. My driving lessons ended, and now I was frustrated again as this freedom were taken from me. All I had at my disposal was a pushbike, walking, or travelling via buses. So I travelled away from my home on the weekends as much as possible. I did not care where I went; I just had to escape, so I did. I would travel to wherever using whatever excuses I could find to just run away from the life I had to try to get some peace and soul comfort. So with me finally being allowed to leave home, my parents' luck had run out and I no longer gave a shit. I needed out of that situation in any way I knew how.

Two of the most traumatic situations and the catalyst for my leaving town occurred a day before my deb ball. These occasions were rather close together.

The first occurrence was when I was walking home in broad daylight. One of my brother's scummy drug-related mates picked me up. At the time, sweet mentally innocent me had no real understanding about drugs, but I knew they existed, and I had seen a small amount of pot in a matchbox at school once. I knew more about alcohol than other drugs. But now in hindsight, I knew this was a person who partook of drugs often, probably hard drugs also, and he had that devious look about him—jeans, black shirt, shaved head covered in tattoos; you know the type. However, I was blind to this at the time. This guy asked me if I would like a lift to my place; he was going there to see my brother, or so he said. I had seen him before, and he would have gone to school with my brother, so he was maybe twenty-one by this stage. I figured it would be OK. Instead of driving me home, however, he drove me out to a creek about three kilometres from home and told me to fork it or walk it, which meant have sex with him or I would have to walk the whole way home. I walked the entire way home, and he stopped every now and then to chase me around the white utility truck that he owned, hoping that he could have sex with me. He would get back in his car, and I would keep walking, with him driving beside me, trying to convince me to have sex with him.

I walked the whole way home. I was hot, angry, scared, and really pissed off, as these now-frequent occurrences where becoming more and more serious and harder to control. Yelling at my brother in front of my parents, telling them how scared I was, was of no use. They just did not wish to know. I could have talked until I was blue in the face, as it made not an ounce of difference in my life. My brother, with his now-so-common flippant "don't give a shit" attitude towards me, quickly turned the conversation around to make it a subject of my stupidity. Not his constant barrage of sexual slurs heralded out of a fast-moving car but my poor judgement at the time, of a guy he considered a scumbag. Hateful and nasty were the words which he commonly used to distort my character, all to shape and the criminal's own assumptive report of the situation so he came out looking so innocent of any wrong doing.

My shoulders so broad now the balancing act of sorts, of the two prominent men in my life my character did they wrought so he proudly gave his assessment of this guy. The only one who really seemed to count in this situation was his opinion, so it must be true. It had nothing to do with the fact that he had crushed and destroyed every boundary protection barrier I was ever born with—no, of course not, nothing to do with that at all. I guess I was just to the breaking point of the inability to even have any say on how I was to be treated and that none of my opinions of my brother and his treatment of me would hold any weight whatsoever with my mother, who had helped groom this man into the smart-ass cocky little cunt he was. Then there was the father who was so oblivious, or so I thought, of everything except his business, and refused to see him as anything but a shining example of good parenting and a shining example of someone to take over the business before he died. But exactly which business was he going to take over, not realizing that more than one business had been operating in front of my eyes?

The final straw and the thing that made me leave town was the guy who pinned me down in the main town park one night as I walked home through the edge of the park. If it were not for the police pulling up to one of my brother's mates on the road about twenty-five metres from where he had me pinned that night, I am confident that the rape that had started would have been completed. As the siren pieced the night sky and momentarily blocked the noise of the passing Thursday night traffic, blue and red flashing lights came on, flooding the leaves of the trees that were sheltering us from the road, and the guy freaked. He jumped up as if springing to attention on to his feet and ran off so quickly. Left alone and picking myself up, fixing my clothes and coming out of the part of the park where this had happened to sit on the stools, I was left stunned, relieved that I was not harmed and recoiling from what had happened. I watched as the police wrote a ticket to the owner of the car during the next twenty minutes or so.

I just sat there on the stool as they charged my brother's friend with whatever he had done wrong in the car he was driving, a white Commodore, I believe from memory. Tears came to my eyes with the realization of what had taken place and the possible consequences—and how the universe saved my already crushed soul from that experience as well. I continued my disturbed journey to take a shortcut home. After this, I was desperate to leave town. I did not care how; I just wanted out. My stupid fucking parents did not give a shit what happened to me, so I needed to flee. I went to a relative's home, and it still puzzles me that I actually saw my mother crying for the first time ever when she said I could go live with them, our relative and her husband. She cried about it as though her conscience, which she had ignored my whole life until then, seemed to kick in and she finally tried to do something to help me out of this situation she had a great hand in creating. I had been prepared to leave with the sideshow when they left town, just to get the fuck away from this absolutely frustrating situation where I had absolutely no control over my life by now. Hopefully, I could finally feel somewhat safe away from my brother and his family, my so-called family. I wanted peace at last from the world I had known and been forced to live in, with little to no rights of my own.

After I left home, my dream girl took on a different feel and a different adventure. I escaped to my auntie's home and lived with her, beginning to unfold the torment that had been my life. I had no idea what to do. I just knew I was numb and had no real comprehension of the world around me except that I no longer had that fucking cunt of a brother in my life. I had moved away and was free of the bullshit, and I began to sculpt a new and different life, one that no longer had the torment of being mentally and emotionally abused every day. I drew a skull at the age of eighteen, for that's how I saw myself or, more to the point, I couldn't feel there was anything left resembling who I actually was, as I was dead inside. That which could be called my true self was buried so deep and mostly I had been trained like a performing monkey as far as how to feel; and how to behave; and not to feel anything that may bring into question anything that was my possession of ownership to me. So after fleeting to my aunties I was blessed to finally begin my life when I moved into my first dwelling of my own. My flat was mine, and the life I lived was quiet and content for the first time in my life.

The dream girl began a different life from the one when she had been trapped in that house with no control over anything in her life. She finally had been allowed to drive away, and that little car had taken her away from the home she had grown up in and the disastrous start to life she was made to endure under her captives' roof, being prisoner of a sick fuck and held there under duress, with no control over anything except the fear and terror she possessed. So upon finally escaping and moving away from my family, I was able to begin the task of healing, not that I understood that at the time that that was what I was beginning to do. I was just so happy to be away from my fucking child molesting family. Once the excitement of this new life began to get into a rhythm, my dream girl turned up again in my dreams and began to live a different life. I had moved by now into a small flat of my own and was working more consistently on a routine of working, housework, friends, and fun.

As I carved out a life from the pain that was mine, my dream girl began to walk a different stride. She now lived in a trailer park; her new home was on wheels, and she lived in a caravan, alone and concealed. The freeness she felt from her comings and goings was quite different from that which she'd known. She now befriended an old woman who lived in the caravan park as well; her wheels were more permanent but evident still. She began to read tarot cards, her table seen well and clear by all passes by, as my dream girl walked past her night after night as my dreaming continued along this new path. She sat there as the years drifted by, always asking to read what I had wished to hide. Never obliging to stop but a minute, this old woman all wrinkled and withered from ages all alone in that sweet little van, little possessions without a man. No one visits and no one to come home to, just this old woman who sits all alone. Her tormented eyes were never disguised, and my dream girl stared into her same knowing eyes. The life in the caravan park was very peaceful, and I found that this old woman was forever asking my dream girl to read her tarot cards as she would walk past her caravan and see her table set up. Night after night, this dream sequence played, as the years drifted by. She only stopped to be polite and have a small chat with this old woman, who seemed content and was continually asking to see if she could read my dream girl's tarot cards.

The young girl of my dreams was sneaking past every night, never really stopping to ask what was right. She just observed the old woman's craft as the cards they did lay, to a carrier of fortune telling of what is her dismay, her mystic world that her character portrayed. Her hands were withered as she stood in that small doorway, so wanting to impart her gifts of knowledge my way, of my next life path and what it portrayed. This old woman was battered in life; to no real love had she been exposed; only the lust that served to disgust. Very much seen as old and battered, of what in her life did she find that really mattered, grey hair the years of wisdom all there, as it was easy to see that life had taken its toll. The payment was made, and many years had gone by. As this old woman beckons so, she visits me nightly in my dream world; wishing to do a reading, never realizing the extent of the gifts in revealing what's to come. The girl of my dreams was too scared to inquire as she sneaked past each time the distant world of her childhood behind her.

10
CHAPTER

The only comfort from my mother was "You've made your bed, now lie in it." The strange thing was, I made nothing. I didn't make this bed; others had and now I was made to lie in it. The situation that was created was all blamed on me—that this was of my making—when in fact it was not. The spiteful words spat at me, placing all the blame on me—that the situation that had developed was of my doing. The angry demeanour that I had clothed myself in as protection was beginning to harden around my heart. This hardened attitude had definitely changed from the once-sweet little girl that I was, transforming me into one who was very pissed off. This hardened exterior I held was more from the harsh way that I had been treated all those years, never allowed to have that soft place to fall but treated so hard and unkind in almost every way of my life.

This hardness with which I had been treated for many years became the pattern that I held—well, not really holding on to but just possessing because I had not been treated any other way in order to know that there was a gentler way to treat myself and thus a better way to conduct myself. Now with this came the fact that the way I talked was also very harsh. I don't mean the words I said; I mean the harsh, strong tone that your voice takes on as it vibrates the anger that is in your body. Over the years, as I have healed from all this, I have seen the tone of my voice change about four times and noticed every time that the tone was getting softer and softer the more I healed. It coincided with my forgiving myself as the major realization of change kicked in and I realized that this had little to do with me, other than being used and placed in a position of being dominated by these people I was given to by the universe at my birth.

Again, my tone of voice had changed, and it happened so quickly, within seconds, and the change was permanent. I find it almost impossible to go back to the harsh, strong tone of voice I once had, unless an emotion of that time is spoken about, and then I have the tone back it's not really even at the same strength that it once was. It had a gentleness behind it now rather than cold and angry emotions of hatred backing it. Now I also mentions that this is not talking about the words chosen that I spoke but it also affects them as well. I have noticed with this gentleness of speech that comes with healing from this, you start to choose different words to speak. Each word has a different vibrational energy behind it. So if you are speaking and only using words that are harsh, they will all hold the similar vibrational signature and thus contribute to the overall vibration of your body. So yes, I also have noticed over this time frame of forty years that the words I have chosen to speak have also been ones of a gentler, kinder, and softer vibrational nature to myself.

This harshness that I possessed meant that I was treating myself rough and very hard, but that was only because I had only been treated this way; therefore, I felt it was normal. Hence, this is the type of man that I was attracted to; the ones that only treat you harshly and also speak with a harsh tone. Thus they tend to break their toys, but now you're one of their toys and you break just like the others. By now, I had moved closer to the big city, and I was in a relationship with a young man who had also had a train wreck of a life. We therefore seemed quite well matched for disaster. Pushing myself harder and longer than most while putting up with a situation that most people would have long walked away from, I stayed because I'd learned to endure such harsh cruelness. So I stayed in this relationship for too long instead of honouring myself. I endured punishment, just as I had been taught.

Another symptom of this harsh behaviour I was subjected to by my child molesting family was that this hardness in my persona meant that I treated everything with the same harshness with which I had been treated. Things began to break under my hands because there was very little gentleness in my life. I was unaware of how hard I had become. My possessions would break because I had been treated with such a heavy hand of hatred that that was the only thing I knew.

I found that instead of placing things down gently, I set them down hard on surfaces, banging and clanging, and as they made contact, they would shatter, a lot like the way I was treated. As my personality shattered, so did my possessions, as the weight at which I was controlled was of such force that I had no option but to comply. For a long time, I was angry that I had been given a defective radio or gift, never a good one, as mine would always break and not work properly after a while. I thought for a long time that someone must have been breaking my things deliberately, and sometimes they had, but mostly because of the harsh way I was treated, I was angry and hard on everything, mirroring the way I was treated. Thus I didn't know any other way to behave. Broken things not working properly was something that I got used to, and in turn it made my life harder and more frustrating, as I would have to spend money to buy another one or put up with the broken item. I never truly had nice things, for I felt I didn't deserve them, as I had been told as a child that I did not deserve a goddam thing. Things I bought would not stay pristine for long. They soon would have chips, dints, and marks on them, torn and tarnished, resembling the way I now behaved and the way I perceived myself inside and portrayed out into the world of the way I had been treated.

I have learned that with my character, I need to have a new item in my possession for a while without using it at all. I didn't even take it out of the wrapper until I'd owned it for a few months and was beginning to accept that I did indeed deserve this new something in my life. Once you have become accustomed to having this new thing in your life, you will look after it better and not break it. You will treat it OK and respect the new item in your world. This includes shoes, clothes, electrical items, cars, and furniture, and so on. I still allow time to go by before I start using them so I can program my mind that indeed I do deserve these items in my life and am worthy of having them here under my now-gentle control. That yes I am worthy of such an item of procession and that I can indeed look after this item with gentleness and worthiness of ownership.

The way I walked was even hard, and the soldier stiff heels thumping into the pavement sent shudders up my spine. This harsh way of walking made my shoes wear out quickly. Because of this stiff thumping way of walking, my knees ached and I was sore in my vertebra, thus my lower back ached from all the strain of this solider-like walking. Exasperated from all the storing of the pain and anger in the lower parts of my back, also crumpling the discs to compress from years of all these unspoken emotions embedded in my lower chakra centres. I was commanding my body to be harsh and rigid, the muscles tightly holding it all together to prevent it from escaping out of my body and into the world, which would ease all this tension stored in my body.

Because of all this harshness, I found that the foods I chose to eat did not help matters. Choosing foods that fed my addictions that I had employed years earlier to help me cope with the overwhelming stress in my childhood seemed to be turning against me and making me acidic. There was a burning inside my body trying to escape as more and more foods seemed to make me sick. Such foods ultimately made me sicker and sicker, and sinus and breathing problems developed. My lungs were clogged, and the breath of life was squeezed from my body, as my lungs were so constricted, making it difficult to breathe. The lungs of the body have the emotional signature of grief linked to them, not surprising that I had problems in this area of my body. My nose was continuously clogged, and the pain in my head squeezed like a vice, making even my teeth ache. My hands were so cold, and my feet were like ice. I could never seem to get any blood flow to those areas of my body. I continuously ached under the strain of all the mess as my blood became so intoxicated with impurities from the food I had been consuming for years while trying to hold back the dam of anger. My allergies became a constant battle with boxes of tissues, and the hacking of phlegm day after day rang out throughout my home, the blowing of my nose constant. This horrible feeling not only affected me but also my children while I healed from this, and the poor bastard had to be afflicted with a wife who had been violated far too early to emotionally, mentally, and physically develop into this role of a young woman.

I was married and had three children, and I was just wandering through life with no real direction or understanding of what life was about, just that I was constantly sick. I was just falling though time with no rhythm or rhyme, just hoping and praying the tormented mind of blame would tame and soothe my crushed brain. My schooling was just a joke, with no words of note to comprehend just what was written. I started to teach myself to read what was written. I had started to read and learn desperately, devouring anything I could. I studied tarot cards and became a tarot reader of sorts. As the vivid memory of my dream girl floated in and out of my dreams, I began to search for answers that were swimming around my brain.

My life was still a mess, with no understanding of much, just wanting to learn where I could. Adult literacy helped me go back to school, graduating after four long years of correspondence, and a small foundation now took shape. My world was now spinning with facts at my fingertips, eagerly learning to get life's grip. I trolled though pages and pages of stuff, all the while learning the valuable lessons that I missed while growing up. I was so eager to start life and feel as if I belonged, my world now opening up to a very different life's song. All the while, I was starting to live, to require answers to what are truly life's big questions. Life was of such a pace that I could barely keep up, my mind filled with torment, and still I must race. By now in my early twenties I was so frustrated at life and the pattern of events with which had built the foundation of my life I was scrambling for answers to why?

I staggered sheepishly into the counsellor's office and quietly sat down, so scared of everything and so unsure of myself. I blurted out, "Am I in the right place? I have a millions things to say; and I need to talk to someone to help me sort it all out. I am so tormented with life and its pace; I am so lost, with no one to rely on or give me a place. Again I am to stand all alone and I don't know why. My marriage is practically over, three children in tow; I am battered and bruised from this, now I know. I'm still recovering from the scars that conclude yet that again that I'm unloved and unworthy, no more than a punching bag of this latest male rage. My life that I had built again is scattered on a flimsy foundation of no moral code. I'm learning that males make the rules of this world, and still the foundation I built was on a bed of nails. The foundational nails were not truly mine but what others had given me to build on and the foundation I wanted had not been discovered yet. Again I am left with no real security and left to fend for myself, which I have to endure. As the nails of another's foundational principles jabbed me all the time.

"I'm so disillusioned about just what to do. Can you please

help me? I have no idea what to do. The young girl inside is again all scared that I'm uncared for from this now type of abuse. The scar barely healed, still sore to the touch, from the latest debacle, and now worn for life is this new badge of distrust. I am alone, and no one can help; again I must stand, for heaven's sake. I am stronger but battered from living where I did dwell; I breathe a sigh of relief that I escaped from this hell. I feel I've lived a whole life—a lifelong relationship compressed into six— and velocity of this life lesson. I often wondered was I collecting information from a past life lesson in this experience gained, as the words which fell from my mouth were I feel like I've lived a whole life again in this experience as I sit and pull apart just what's been added to the list of self-blame. The third chakra seven year sequences are complete, and now the beginning of the heart chakra will take seven years to complete. I am barely twenty-two, and already I have had more of life's experiences than most they could chart. I am exhausted, but I feel like I'm free—like a bird I can whistle, another ring on my life's tree. I am free for a while again, until I stumble into another relationship of a different degree.

"I am studying and learning and reading quiet a lot. I am beginning to pull apart my life to examine the plot and explore just why I have a life not of my choosing. I have talked for three years now and barely scratched the surface, my life so complex with hidden compartments, the compressed box still closed tight and sealed into darkness. I foolishly think I am finally healed from this stuff and the years of abuse have all been revealed. My life is much better, and I almost complete, with my senior pass my reward for no defeat.

My dream girl hovered in the background most of the time, never really bothering me much. When this relationship ended and I had three children in tow, it was here that my dream girl made her reappearance back into my dreams more prominently. The old woman was still there and still she beckoned me to read my cards. I guess I will never know what made her say yes. Maybe it was I, who was ready to grow, and I was finally in a safe place to do so, but she agreed to this old woman reading her cards. I recall the cards as they were shuffled and placed on the table, with the cards beginning to turn over, which was not the focus of this night. My dream girl stood just to the side of the doorway as the cards on the tale top began to turn in the old woman's hand, and as the back of the first card hit the table, revealing the face of that first card, the woman transformed in front of my eyes.

She was no longer the frail old woman but a strong and confident person standing there with an eagle's head where her head should sit, its feathers of white flowing over the chest of this warrior. The stance of a formidable creature with the legs of an Indian warrior stood in front of her, my dream girl, no questioning of confidence and strength. She was a warrior of sorts, strong and fierce, standing there with immovable strength and integrity, ready to fight any battle placed in front of her, to fight alongside my dream girl. But within seconds, she then transformed into a beautiful blonde woman, graceful and gentle and well protected a glow of self-strength and love as her beautifully flowing blonde hair drifted down over her body, covered in a white flowing dress, her shoulders concealed with hair. Her grace and elegance conveyed not the once-damaged frail woman beaten down with life, guilt, and distress but the core strength of a healed soul, so strong and confident that she was able to protect herself from harm.

Within seconds, the images were gone, but they were burned forcefully into my soul's memory, the images so real and alive that I woke up shocked and completely surprised that the forceful confidence this dream had left me with was so vivid and stark that my heart was beating strongly in my chest. The warrior woman had been born in my psyche, and I was too oblivious to realize that a transformation of my life had begun in that split second. The flood of strong emotions filled every facet of my body as my awake self-stared up at the ceiling of my room in my modest three-bedroom home, shocked and pulled out of sleep at the velocity of this dream and the click of this mechanism in that one card turning. My life changing forever, when that one card hit that table, face up, and this old woman changed. I was held for years under that one card, and now the card hitting the table with the permission given to read my cards, the trigger of such a powerful dream sequence ricocheting through time twenty-five years in the future. Still reeling from what had happened, I didn't realize at that time that this dream that was over in what seemed a split second had actually given me a glimpse at what my future held and the stages on which my life would take place and the development of my life if I chose to keep going and keep searching for answers. I did not understand it at the time, nor did I realize that my dream that I had had since I was nine was now complete, never to dream it ever again. I was now twenty-five and the single mother of three. The first dream had completed, and the next one would soon come back into the fore ground of my realisation. I never had this dream again, and this one dream that had developed in my sleeping subconscious had escaped into the visions of the night and left, depositing such powerful information of the future and the path that I would take.

My eyes are still obscure to the ways of a man, not seeing the newest reptilian suitor with his own plans, slithering his way into the life that is mine. But to the world I must be a fright, a single mum all weighted down and easy to slay; I have come on the radar as a different prey. I'm looking for love, the heart chakra is so starved, the heart sequence in play, so I am searching for love and comfort in any disguise; my judgement is off, my eyes are not clear of why this one is love, I had no idea. Is it because to my ears he spoke so gently? Or was it that he knew just what to say, schooled in the right repertoire of words so I was easy prey!

"More lies and deceit, the truth never known, what the real issue is, to me never known. My time is taken up with raising kids and now there are six, schooling, study, and the home that we made. As the years drifted by, I was able to take stock of my life once more, employing strategies that would make me so complete and the enduring scar of my life so young and mistreated, a mark forever embedded into my soul and now burned complete. The separating of me from my supposed family was a blessing, as I repaired the damage this family had in their messing. I began to feel a little better as I worked out who I was to become for the better. I have learned to be a gentle parent to myself finally. I continued to change my behaviour lovingly; this time the bending and the changing were done by me, the reconstructing of the soul, my abilities done. I turned to religion to get a good foundation of what a family really should be. I found this interesting, as this also comes with its problems, but at least I had something of a gauge to live by now and I could see lots of families and how they were supposed to conduct themselves together and work as a complete unit, which I had never had in my life." There was the stark reminder in seeing these families, that I was forced to put up with all this shitty behaviour, as you see families of all sorts in this environment. It became a great training ground for me to mirror what a true family looked like and behaved like.

While growing up in your family, I taught myself to control my body so I didn't feel and didn't respond to any sexual act being forced upon me; the only real way I knew how to respond is just to turn it off and protect my innocence, along with most other things that in the process get switched off also. When I eventually did start to unfreeze and unwrap years later in adulthood from the tight ball of guilt control I had become, I found that life hummed along in its own fashion, while I was again oblivious to the charade behind the curtain I never saw. I was busy with trying to study at UNI, working, family, and sorting out the problem at hand, which was my desire to be somewhat normal. This normality desire also found its way into my bedroom that I thought I shared with my husband.

I began to wish to grow sexually on my own terms so to achieve this I found a strategy to use while in the bedroom. It was better for me to focus on a book of sexual poetry first. It would be one that described how the act of true lovemaking is gentle and sensual instead of the cold, demanding forcible hand reaching into your soul to steal the last bit of goddam goodness from whichever position you are manipulated into performing. The poetry book allowed my brain to program how I was meant to see this act and then slowly move into whatever I was supposed to do, going extremely slow to start with, until I reprogrammed myself that it was safe and OK to feel good about this. Training my mind to stay present in my body was not an easy thing while I allowed someone to share this space with me and share my body willingly, without running scared into another place, the one I had successfully retreated to as a child when things got too bad to look at.

However, this is not when my body unfroze and began to exhibit normal sensations that one should have, such as a feeling of arousal and sexually turned on, as it was still stuck like concrete and dead of any feeling, as it had been trained years earlier to behave. The connection between head and body had still not been re-established as yet. I realized that because of the abuse I had received as a child, I had to have my partner pleasure me first, rather than me pleasing him first. As if I had started first pleasuring him, this would have been the same pattern being re-enforced during my abuse and I needed to change the pattern, as I would not be able to function with the necessary relaxation if I was forced to start pleasuring him like when I was abused. My abuse always started with me having to pleasure him, so I changed the behaviour. I was reminded constantly that this was a chore I once had to perform and not the pleasurable act of two people who wish to share their closeness with the other in the bond of lovemaking. Most people miss the spiritual connection of two people that results in the deep connection of passion, choosing the superficial release of bodily fluids instead, with two people who don't really care for each other; it's superficial lust at best.

On my journey, I had to reprogram myself with good sexual experience, ones that were developed over time with love and respect for the other. I had to take the time to allow my body to catch up to my mind and allow my body the respect to switch back on, which has taken forty years to happen. See, over many years, you teach yourself to switch off physical sensations you are not supposed to have but also turned off in a way to protect yourself from everything else being taken from you, and then you are expected to flick a switch and turn it back on; it doesn't work like that. So I had to give myself time for my body to adjust to the feeling that what my mental programming said was wrong and that I was now telling my body that it was OK. This takes time and patience but hang in there, for it eventually comes back. But you need a man who has reached the depths of true lovemaking and understands the deeper emotional connection to help you, not the superficial man-boy just after a poke to satisfy his shallow needs.

Memories when they are clouded with bad ones too numerous to count, taking the time to implant good ones to take their place, is vitally important, but can take time and patience. I can say that after years of trying, I now have some wonderful memories instead of the crappy ones that were forced upon me. So be extremely gentle and loving with yourself, finding someone who will be willing to take this journey with you. Taking the time to stop if you need to and just allow yourself to open up at your pace—no rush but a gentle loving process of self-discovery, which you were not able to do naturally because you were forced long before your time. Stopping when you lose it, and practice remaining in your body during the experience rather than separating and running to your special place. This can be much harder and take longer than it took to write these words on this page.

Oblivious to what was going on, my children, now teenagers all of a sudden, and I found myself no longer being allowed to say in my home. I was kicked out and had four children not realizing just why it all went wrong, as I was focused on everything, thinking that life was good and we were getting all we needed in life. Bills were being paid, and my career was starting. I was beginning to see how I could bring some real money into this family through running my own business. But all of a sudden it was over and I was out, twelve years of marriage dissolved in one short time frame: "Get out. You and your children are no longer of use to me." This marriage ended, and for a long time, I just did not see the realization of what I had been involved in. My body was sick real sick, and it took many years to recover from what I had been giving it over the years. My hair fell out, my body was starved of nutrients, and I was recovering from a drug addiction that I did not even realize I even had.

I remember the counsellor telling me that one of my blessings was that I did not know what it was I had been given and thus could not get a fix for something I did not know I took. I almost walked out when she said I had an addiction to a substance, but she was aware that I had no idea that it existed. Alone again and staring out the window of my new dwelling I now lived in, I was scared and recovering from this next dilemma. I had to just pack up and walk away from everything, start again anew so nothing of my former life could come through. Changing everything—and I mean everything—is a scary thing. You don't realize that all these little things you own and take possession of make you secure in life. All the little possessions that are yours, all the places you go, and the creature comforts that make your life just so. But I had to walk away from everything, and I found that the only way to retreat was to put my battered life back into the hands of the people who had allowed it to be destroyed years earlier. It's a hard thing to have to crawl back to these people knowing you have no one else to turn and you're so sick and crushed again, vulnerability screaming out, but what other choice did I have? It took about eight years to recover from that experience, not realizing just what it meant and how that large piece to the puzzle fit into the whole story of why my life had been so controlled, manipulated, and manoeuvred so I never truly got what I wanted. Instead, I was used and manipulated into service in one way or another by my family and their associates.

Over this time, after I had healed from all the mess my last husband left me with, I graduated UNI and started my business. I began to discover my own body, and yes, I had four children who were almost grown now but had remained frozen in time, with very little understanding of the way I was meant to feel or behave normally in my body in a world of being in a bedroom. The tight little ball of fear that controlled that part of me sexually was still operating quite well, and I was reluctant to try anything that left me with the feeling of being not in control of what happened to me in my experience with sex now. Having to force my body not to respond to what was being done to me all those years ago was something that I could not just turn off and on, for which I still did not realize had still not been released and unfrozen, due to being manipulated chemically forced stimulation via me being drugged and not real bodily relaxation. So all the progress which I thought I had made in unfreezing my body was not real progress at all but had been manipulated via chemical to stimulate the adrenals to over produce sexual hormones and thus feeling of arousal in my vagina, and thus when I had detoxed the chemicals out of my body the resulting factor was I was still back to where I originally was with very little ability to experience true mind body connection, sexually.

So now my life was somewhat back in the hands of these people that I fled from when I was a teenager, and I did not really have much to do with these people my family for my family's protection. But again, where else could I have gone? I had few friends, and most of the people I did know, were my last partners support system friends, so I was again on my own with four teenagers in tow, and I had to try to find some security for them. Out of the little respect for my mother that I had, I tolerated my family but chose never to allow them to talk openly about my brother to me. I just did not wish to know about him or the fabulous life he was living while I was trying to build a foundation of something good under my feet faster than everyone was trying to destroy it underneath me. I was never bending or complying with gestures of reconciliation towards him and his family. I was forever waiting to see if he had changed, but with his inability to bend and take responsibility for his past actions, there was just stark refusal on his part that he had even done anything wrong.

So I had no other option than to take this to court and find someone who would show him the errors of his attitude and ways and force him to bend in realization that he should never have done what he did to me. He needed to apologize to me. I now sit patiently waiting for time to tick by so the time is just right. This is incredibly difficult after waiting for forty-three years for someone to do something, and I guess, if I am honest with myself, I always knew it would have to be me who took the lead and changed the world, my world. My father did not intend to change anything. Why would he? Life would be perfect if only I would shut the fuck up, be a good little girl, and sit in my corner and say nothing. While in the background, they manipulated my life to get what they wanted to hide their grubby little world.

11
CHAPTER

I had not seen him for many years let alone talked to this man whom they referred to as my brother and I no longer did. I had not for many, many years now considered this man as any part of my family. He was just a person whom lived in the house I grew up in and had sexually abused me for many years. With the comings and goings of the nurses and the staff of the nursing home, here I was the bed between me and my father and him, my sexual molester, the only protection from this family. Here I was, with her dying in front of me, my mother was dying and I had to put up with him being in the same room while she passed away in the nursing home where she had been living for some years now. Look what you had to do my wife to get the family back together my father said and the disbelief hit my ears of what he was focused on. All happy that he had dodged a bullet and not had to deal with the pending atonement of sins he knew his son had committed along with himself. I was standing by myself again, all on my own in a room with my family, something I was no longer accustomed to after some twenty-five years. I limited him, my sexual molester, with the amount of bullshit I would be subjected to from this parasite of a person. I had not allowed him into my world for years, and I liked it that way. I stared at him, the once formidable figure that had control of my complete soul all those years ago, standing in front of me.

No love lost and clearly not ashamed or remorseful for anything which he had done to me, he just did not care. Hard pill to swallow while standing in front of a man whom destroyed your life and stole so much from you and clearly by the not very humble attitude, thinking he did not need to change, nor did he feel that he had to. It grated on my nerves that day in the nursing home where my mother had been living. Knowing I had to bite my tongue and say nothing was excruciating and exhausting but strength of character held me true, as this was bearable compared to some things I had had to endure. It would have been of little value to open my mouth at such a time, as the outcome would not have altered anything.

I feel I fought well that day to stand my ground and not crumble into the little girl he once had total control over. He was visibly unnerved by the way old tactics once used to control me, no longer worked on me, and his longing for the jabs of venomous sarcasm for pending victory; did not come. Only comforted by our father whom he relied on to hold steady and never betray him, he is the golden child and I was just scum. He no longer controlled me and I felt strong, even though my mother lying there dying in front of me was weighting heavy. I was determined that day that I would win this battle of wills and be stronger than ever against this parasite of a man, who had once held my precious emotional, physical, mental existence in his depraved hands. Hence, the only strategy I found I could use to heal my tormented body and mind from these people who had forced control of my body into the hands of this man was to segregate myself away from them. My children had never met him and thankfully did not know him, and over the years of counselling and kilometres of written words to rid myself of his control over my body and mind, I had succeeded in regaining the control over my soul, once stolen from me.

Although my father had tried to wipe the floor clean with his comment, of having the family back together, I did not allow it to be that way. To try and gain my ground back, for which my father was trying to sweep away in the events of my mother's passing in the nursing home that day. I was able to use the newspaper article both my father and brother were discussing as my platform. As I listen to their discussion of the subject matter in the paper that day, I was able to bring to both their attention in a quiet room of the nursing home, that what they were talking about referred to our family as well. When finally...a break immerged in their verbal mudslinging of the prominent churches handling of child sexual abuse cases, happened. I took my shot and was very accurate in its delivery; a powerful blow of honest reality check was given. Not nasty or sarcastic just down right matter of fact that – no the family is not back together and this is why! Nothing got said as they both got up in unison and left the room wordless and leaving me behind with the desired results, balls still in play. My father knew it had not finished by my comment and that his balls were still on the chopping block as well as his son's.

I was stronger, yet the dynamic dance of the characters in the room that day still played out. My mother was dying! We had become closer as the final years of her life played out. The countless integration of her wanting answers tired me on occasion as she pieced together the truth from the lies she had been told. I tried to have feeling for this woman but only stood as if a client of mine was passing away in front of me, as I held my body staunchly at having to be in the same room as this vile man who had been such a bastard to me. My child molester, having the same don't-give-a-fuck-about-you attitude, was not talking to me, as if I was of no consequence anyway, just like when I was young.

I stood there evaluating this man and waiting to see if his ego had humbled any in regards to the subject of what he had considered his right of passage in our family. Nothing, just the same bastard that he had always been, and with the cruel I-don't-give-a-fuck-about-you, attitude, nothing had changed. Nothing had changed in all those twenty-five years of life. Had he even stopped to evaluate what he had done to me in all that time? Did he even care that what was allowed to be done to me was wrong? Had he stopped during even one heartbeat to consider just how his cruel behaviour had destroyed the very essence of me? My breaths were very shallow as my mind remained in my body, keeping my emotions in check. I would command my body and thoughts and how they behaved at this time. I was not going to relinquish any of my self-control to him, as I was the captain of my ship and the setter of my life's sails now.

As this woman passing away in front of me happened I was reminded of a thought that I was adopted, for that's the only explanation of such abuse at the hands of this family when I was young that I could conceivably have for it to have happened. She was a woman unable to talk or move, and I often wonder if she could have talked, what she would have said to me. And would it have come from a place for my comfort or hers? The years of this saga were now developing in front of me as I held my ground that day in that room of the nursing home as my mother died. I was triumphant in the knowledge that I was a strong person and this was not how a family was supposed to behave. Here I was forty years later still confidently holding onto the attitude that the behaviour towards me was wrong. That fucking attitude of mine has never change that this was and is wrong to treat a family member with child sexual abuse or anyone on the earth for that matter.

It was her last breath as a woman, and here I was, making sure she was comfortable, with her needs met and my just walking through the steps until she died. When it was over, I left, glad to get out of that fucking room with these people who were so full of hate and spitefulness that it left me exhausted holding myself on guard around them, waiting for them to pounce. I walked away and was grateful that I could escape to my place of work and throw myself into my work as a distraction. I was grateful that I did not have to be around them anymore and could get back into a safe environment, which meant I could get out from behind the shield of protection I had been wearing while my mother died.

12
CHAPTER

The violent shaking of the spinal cord the day that it released, all the trapped, compressed mess of hatred that was blocking and holding back the free flow of love energy deep down in my soul. I could feel it trapped there for years and the exploding of energy shooting up my spine and expelling in twisted existence for the universe to take possession of, leaving this bodily world and freeing my body of hatred. I felt vulnerable, empty, and finally at peace as my limp body, which had been held frozen in time, was emptied and the cork of spiteful lustful hate given to me all those years ago was finally expelled from my life. My love energy was now able to flow freely, and I could now feel the results physically in my body. The cocoon of time broke open for the butterfly to finally emerge, and I am now pumping life into my wings as I learn to expand love into each and every facet of my soul. I can physically feel the free flow of energy up and down my chakra centres, as the energy is no longer blocked.

For years, my angry persona stood as my protection, trying to sort out this twisted mess. The powerful stance of my Indian warrior, with hands folded over chest and an eagle head, was dominant in my life, vigilant that I was protected against this harsh world of unscrupulous men and the no care given of the damage they bring into the world, contributing to its destruction. I understand now why I was given such a dominant figure on which to base my persona. It was protecting me all these years that I have been healing my broken soul from this choking smog poisoning me, protecting the innocent young woman I was as his strong integrity-based belief system, strong in its character of what was right and wrong, stood guard over my soul. Something was clearly missing from my childhood because the men in my life had little decent character and were only out to control and destroy, to fulfil their selfish needs without regard.

This guardian of my soul was there, quietly standing guard for years as I grew into the woman I am today. I never realized she was there or what it meant as I developed in areas that would allow me to expand and grow, my physical, mental, and emotional body becoming strong and the core centre of my soul whole for the first time. I never truly understood what they meant when people would talk about strengthening your core. My understanding of my core of my body was not even a concept yet. However, I now know that it was there and what it was to represent. The understanding that your spinal cord is a real organ in its own right and that I can strengthen it and make it strong. The now realisation, that the wispy unnourished energy that was there in my central nervous system, in the core of my spine, was supposed to keep me strong but was very weak, almost non-existent to my awareness, and thus, because it had never been truly strong and nourished, it never occurred to me that it was weak and not really functioning to full capacity. But that day, my spinal cord shook and all the violent verbalizing of past angry unvoiced confrontations escaped from so deep down in my body that it ripped the roots of my family tree out and expelled them from my body.

The violent shaking, the energy of this vibrating ball of trapped energy pierced through all the layers of pain overlaid year after year, taking with it all that no longer belonged inside of me. I was emptied of all the spiteful, hateful nastiness ever given me. I was free, and the vibrational change flung me across time and space, into a gentle place of love, as the emergence of the beautiful blond women emerged from under the rubble that had held my essence to life. The exploded force required to break open the cast irons which held, hateful bands that had been suffocating my heart and shattering the bonds of this hateful male control over my soul was liberating. It was gone, and the essence of love could now find a home to develop in my soul. The cord of my core existence shook for three days, and as the structure that held my soul was no longer carrying the repulsive twisted vindictive hatred that was given me by my child molester years earlier, I could relax.

It was gone, this blockage that I could feel stuck in my body, held there with no way to move it. It had been there for years, and I knew it, but no amount of reading, writing, or seminars of emotional healing was going to move it. It was trapped firm, deep in my soul, and a force of equal note needed to move it was required, as it had been concreted in my lower chakra soul over years of having to swallow the pain and frustration of turning wrong into right. It was not until I opened my mouth and poured all the content of my soul out to the police that this angry energy exploded from my body and I was free. The emptying of one's trapped soul energy is quiet horrific, but at the same time, a nothing less is experienced as this energy now rushes to escape. You're unable to control it, as the trapped explosive energy has a mind of its own. It was pouring out of me, spewing all the contents of that time forty years ago into the air, expelled and no longer in me but forcibly released in one great gush of energy, instead of the gentle releasing day after day to nourish my soul. I would love to say that physically I felt great, and I did for a short while, but then deep core emptiness developed as the exploding pustules of hatred left my body. It was now cleaned of all hatred but a hole of extreme size was left in the place where all my trapped sexual experience had been forced to store.

For months, this deep core emptiness hung in my psyche, and no amount of trying filled this enormous gap that had been left in my soul. For a while, there was a deep ache of sorts that I wished this had not happened to me and left me vulnerable to the world without an understanding of who I was now. I had changed, and everywhere I looked, I questioned everything as the now-free energy flowed gently through my body and began to fill the facets of empty space gaps that were there. The enormous gap that was left was in part from the trapped energy held down there in my soul in the lower chakra and making my hips bulge, but it was now gone. The only thing I found that would relieve this agonizing empty feeling was to shake. I found that the wobbled machine I used daily was one of the only strategies that seemed to work. This daily shaking of the spinal cord seemed to soothe the empty feeling I was experiencing in my body. All the other strategies I processed were one's designed to keep that fucking energy right where it was, suppressed. But now, with it gone and this hole in my existence empty, I needed to fill it with something that resembled supportive energy to strengthen my self-esteem. I definitely needed to steer clear of alcohol at this time, as I knew it would be a downfall to me had I started to drink alcohol to again suppress these changes that had taken effect and left me with this strange and uneasy feeling in my psyche.

Empty and untormented should have been great, one would think, for this is what I wanted. I no longer had that blocked feeling deep down in the second chakra, but now this free flow of energy was a whole other beast to come to terms with. It's taken a while for me to understand just what this trapped energy immobilized in me. It's hard to express in words just what this lack of nourishing energy doesn't do for you. I feel whole for the first time, but those are just words. What does it really mean in terms of comprehending something into comprehensible words for you to understand? When the energy was not flowing, I felt disjointed in my body. Some parts of me worked, but the nourishment of spirit was just not there. I existed but was not fully nourished in body to take on the world. The strength I feel now is incredible, and a strength is along the entirety of my spinal cord, not just in some places and vacant in others but is now fully complete and strong. Until that released, I could not have told you that I had this sensation of not being fully nourished spinally for my soul, but now I can.

What does the word *beautiful* really mean? The word bounced around in my mind for such a long time, with no real place for it to land. I mean, there was never a place built for it to sit and become part of my existence. The concept that I could be beautiful was never voiced at all while growing up, so how could something so simple, which most women take for granted, not exist in my soul? It had no place to land, to help nourish my heart, unless someone told you when you were young that you were beautiful and placed in you that area that would allow you to hold these words for you to have the understanding of. What a concept that I could be beautiful, and as the now-men I grew up with at school started to say this to me that night, I found it increasingly hard to understand this word as it clanged around the internal recesses of my brain. What could they see that I was not seeing? I heard these words, but they held no value to me at all. I had scarcely heard it at all for most of my fifty-year life, and now, during my school reunion, I was told this continually over the weekend. For the first time, I stared into the mirror, and I found, to my astonishment, that the beautiful woman staring back at me was *me*. The devastated little girl was now gone, and as I stared in this mirror that hung on the wall, I saw a beautiful slim blonde staring back at me from my reflection. I have a little shelf in my soul now to place these words that I hear. I hear it quite often now. A seemly strange shift has been made, and for the first time, I am hearing it and beginning to know that I have a place to put that word—and I know that I must be beautiful.

The ugliness of hatred and lust that penetrated my soul all those years ago was now gone and given back to the person who owned it. This chasm of empty space that normally is filled with love, acceptance, and understanding—of being beautiful and loved—was empty of all the spiteful and nasty twisted concept of no love given. The vast empty expanse of soul was now able to have a whole shelf assigned to "beautiful" and could be built and each and every time I was told this word, it is now added to this brand-new shelf, only months old in my soul. It was something my ears were definitely not accustomed to hearing, but now I have a place for them to live in my soul, while men of all types are saying it, so I am just accepting it that they must know. These nourishing words are like water to a parched soul as the tiny water droplets of love and acknowledgement are slowly seeping into the drought-ridden parts of my heart. This concept of being beautiful is taking hold.

The image of the old woman reading the tarot cards comes to mind, and I often wonder if I didn't now have the burning desire to strive for something better, but with the knowledge that there was something better, I just could not get my hands on it. Would I today be that woman, the plump old woman standing in the doorway of the caravan annex, starring out at the world, waiting to be acknowledged by the passing world, her eyes filled with pain. Poor guilt-ridden lonely old lady, left feeling ugly, that the world is such a horrible place, with no real love ever received from anyone, as this old lady was so starved of everything and strategizing ways to get her needs met without harming anyone. Stuck in an impossible situation with no escape ... Was this what my life was to become, and was my dreaming showing me this glimpse into the world beyond the pain? The world that had been absent from my life is now beginning to find a resting place in my mind as the concept, that I, me, the damaged little girl, could actually be beautiful and thus loved by the world at large.

As I said, physically the scars are hidden from the world, but they are there. They are crumpled up in one great mess, the cruel hatred energy in exchange for my love, forced upon me when I was so young. The love was sucked out of me, leaving me a shell of a person when I was only fourteen, leaving me needy and empty after years of having to supply lust-driven sexual gratification to my brother, who should have never been given the permission to have taken such from me. It was slavery, being forced to give, give, and give until I scarcely had anything for myself. I was sucked dry of any goodness and nourishment as the vacuum was connected to my soul. He began to manipulate the situation so his needs were met and mine were diminished. It's this vacuumed soul that I would drag back to my hole and try to find ways to fill my soul bucket up. The bucket was just raped and forcibly taken advantage of, while my bucket of love and self-acceptance became smaller and smaller as the years progressed. This small area of my soul had nothing left once captured and the contents squeezed and so repeatedly emptied that nothing remained except the shell of a person I was.

Discarded now, I was angry that all my defences were gone. I was vulnerable and handed to the world. This platform on which to build my life was a flat wisp of nothing less but a foundation of quicksand, changing circumstances designed to leave me vulnerable and unable to build a life of quality. I felt stuck over here on this side of the wall, the one that was sleazy and grimy and the only men that existed were all able to take advantage at the drop of a hat because they could see just what had happened to me. I belonged to this side of the great energetic divide, the side of this energetic wall that knows they are doing wrong but continue not to care that they are destroying the world. They are polluting it with painful desires of spiteful loveless lives, raping society of goodness. Their lust for shallow sexual gratification far outweighs any goodness inside them, as they only have eyes driven by hatred and lust. The lowest of vibrations is all they know and the must vibrate to a lowest of vibrations to be allowing this behaviour to continue. Low life's at the lowest level which will eventually have to pass away.

I am on this side of the great divide of souls now. I can now see the great difference in men, and the qualities that drive them are becoming wider and wider as I strive to stay away from them. They are reptilian in nature and driven to steal what they do not possess and have no concept of. They don't experience love forever vacant from their owning. This transformation of my physical body occurred so the wave of self-love trapped in my second chakra was released and took hold, physically transforming my body. I must look like a butterfly released, as so many times I run my hands over my soft skin of my face; the sensation had not been part of my existence before. My fingers tingle as I notice just how soft and smooth my skin is. The gentle energy of love nourishing my psyche now fills my awareness of the energy I was born with, with the parched wilderness of hate dissolving under the weight of loving energy now flowing. The physical acknowledgement of my beauty is now felt on touch.

I guess it goes without saying that when so many things are not given you and are stolen from you, then the parched ground of your existence is all that you are going to have. One other physical thing I have noticed is that my physical heart is weak. Being a muscle of the body, I am well aware that it needs strengthening. It's funny, but it's as if loving energy is being deposited into every cell of my body, and as I experience this phenomenon of sorts, I can physically feel my heart muscle strengthening over time. I feel so much stronger than before. The inner strength that was taken from me many years ago and suffocated over time so they could take possession of my soul is healing.

Another physical difference is my thumbnails, which for years had deep horizontal grooves in them, from one side of my nail to the other. This is a definite sign of deep trauma, and the depth of the grooves is an indication of the trauma endured and for how long. I once had a person tell me that it does not matter if you had something happen once or fifty times; we all feel it the same. Now, on reflection, I am afraid I have to disagree with that statement. If you hit your thumb with a hammer once, you may find that it hurts and you may have a black nail. However, if you hit that same thumb fifty times, I guarantee that the damage to that thumb would be far worse. I have identified that the trauma of this spinal cord energy depletion is shown in the grooves of your thumbnails. The severity of the trauma is shown, and thus the lack of energy free flowing in the core of your person is visible to the naked eye on your thumbnails.

Now, since this energy release has happened, I have watched my nail beds get healthier and healthier. They take anywhere from four to eight months to develop from the nail bed out to the tip, provided they are not chewed short, and the excess of nutrients is given to nail growth. So with this free-flowing energy about two and a half years since the release from the conception until now I, am seeing these thumbnails improve more and more as the time ticks by. Before this time, I could not get my nails to heal, no matter what I did or from the good nutrients from food and supplements I put into my body. But now this nourishing energy that had been blocked for years was working correctly, they are beginning to heal and normalize.

As this change of energy is pumped through the central nervous system of my body on a regular basis, I am getting stronger and stronger. I am able to stand up for myself more and more. The once-trapped unnourished energy could not flow freely and nourish and pick up energy from the other chakras correctly, so I was suffering great deficiency in my personal energy field. The strength of will comes from the third chakra centre, and now that it is not starved of energy, it is beginning to command respect from everyone. I needed to be rather diplomatic here, as for years some people have gotten away with walking over me in ways that I will no longer tolerate. I needed to be gentle in commanding respect in areas where I felt I deserved respect. The boundaries that are connected with chakra two and thus where all this trapped energy was, due to being sexually abused, has now been released. I find that my ability to enforce my newly relinquished boundary system is getting stronger and stronger.

As I push some people back into a healthier area of my life, some are not going to like it, but I don't worry about it. They will get over it, and I will just not give a care. I have been tested with some males, as before they were taking liberties that I was not fully aware they should not be taking, and now I am slowly pushing them back and reinforcing my boundaries as mine, with my right to have them and enforce them how I see fit. I must admit that although this has been the best feeling, it's been the hardest to do, and though they don't like it, I stand firm because it will empower me greatly, knowing that I have the power to protect myself, which was once taken from me. It's now back in my hands, and I am able to voice its clarity of demand.

My understanding now of the crippling of my boundary system in relation to the extent of my sexual abuse was inevitable. They go hand in hand with the development of a person's personal protection structure. So as you are required to suppress all anger of this incident as the sexual abuser disintegrates your boundary, you lose your personal power that is developed in your third chakra centre. It's this personal power that I now feel growing in strength as my boundaries strengthen and give foundational support to the strong structure I am building my life on. My friends who are feeling the same let-down experiences are vigilant in giving me support, and the fact that they are there and thinking of me is of such comfort, not allowing me to be on my own through all this as I was all those years ago, so thank you to the ones who are truly helping.

The collapse of whom I was told to be and the emerging of the phoenix of who I am slowly began to happen, as now the people who put me into this box of behaviour are beginning to squirm under the heat of court. I finally have learned not to care about these people who were my family, and as the incestuous corrosion of the mind heals, I wait for the judgement to take place. Someone asked me if I really care and I had to agree that I couldn't care less about these people, then I stopped and realised I can care less I just need time to learn how. Stay tuned to see what happens next as I explain the next dream and how it developed in unravelling more of my life's puzzle.

Printed in the United States
By Bookmasters